Praise for *The Forgotten Ways*:

"Hirsch has discovered the formula that unlocks the secrets of the ecclesial universe like Einstein's simple . . . formula ($E=mc^2$) unlocked the secrets of the physical universe. There are some books good enough to read to the end. There are only a few books good enough to read to the end of time. *The Forgotten Ways* is one of them."

—Leonard Sweet (from the foreword)

"A full-blooded and comprehensive call for the complete reorientation of the church around mission. Nothing less than the rediscovery of a revolutionary missional ecclesiology will do for Alan Hirsch. A master work."

—Michael Frost, coauthor of *The Shaping of Things to Come* and author of *Exiles*

"Every chapter has the kind of rich insight and inspiring challenge that we have come to expect from Alan Hirsch."

—Brian McLaren, author of *A New Kind of Christian*, *A Generous Orthodoxy*, and *The Story We Find Ourselves In*

"The global mission community is indebted to Hirsch for this seminal book. It is packed with solid exegesis and theological reflection and provides a fresh reading of contemporary Christian authors and a careful evaluation of paradigm-shifting authors from the leadership field. There is rich insight in each chapter for field practitioners and a fresh synthesis of the essentials of biblical missiology."

—Steve Hoke, *Evangelical Missions Quarterly*

"A fascinating and unique examination of two of the greatest apostolic movements in history (the early church and China) and their potential impact on the Western church at the dawn of the twenty-first century. The book may well become a primary reference book for the emerging missional church."

—Bill Easum, Easum, Bandy & Associates
(www.easumbandy.com)

"It is refreshing to read a book related to the missional church that provides theological depth coupled with creative thinking. *The Forgotten Ways* helps to rescue the concept of church from the clutches of Christendom, setting it free to become a dynamic movement in place of a dying institution."

—**Eddie Gibbs,** coauthor of *Emerging Churches: Creating Christian Community in Postmodern Cultures* and author of *LeadershipNext: Changing Leaders in a Changing Culture*

"*The Forgotten Ways* represents the potential that the emergent movement has for the renewal of the whole church. . . . There is very little to disagree with and much to celebrate in this book. Church leaders who desire to mobilize their people for genuine transformational ministry in this postmodern age need to read it."

—**Al Tizon,** *Prism*

"[Hirsch's] reflections are worth reading, reading again and most importantly acting upon. *The Forgotten Ways* is a welcome and significant addition to the literature on mission to the West written by a leading missiological strategist. It will prove to be a useful tool to help shape new forms of missional church—for church planters, those leading change in existing churches and all mission-hearted followers of Jesus."

—**Darren Cronshaw,** *Journal of the American Society for Church Growth*

THE FORGOTTEN WAYS HANDBOOK

A Practical Guide for Developing Missional Churches

ALAN HIRSCH
WITH DARRYN ALTCLASS

Brazos Press

a division of Baker Publishing Group
Grand Rapids, Michigan

Published by Brazos Press
a division of Baker Publishing Group
P.O. Box 6287, Grand Rapids, MI 49516-6287
www.brazospress.com

Printed in the United States of America

Library of Congress Cataloging-in-Publication Data

Hirsch, Alan, 1959 Oct. 24–
    The forgotten ways handbook : a practical guide for developing missional churches / Alan Hirsch with Darryn Altclass.
        p.   cm.
    Companion to: The forgotten ways.
    Includes bibliographical references.
    ISBN 978-1-58743-249-1 (pbk.)
    1. Church. 2. Missions. 3. Postmodernism—Religious aspects—Christianity. I. Altclass, Darryn. II. Title.
BV600.3.H575 2009
266—dc22   2008047968

Published in association with the literary and marketing agency of C. Grant and Company.

The internet addresses, email addresses, and phone numbers in this book are accurate at the time of publication. They are provided as a resource. Baker Publishing Group does not endorse them or vouch for their content or permanence.

This book is dedicated to

The many marvelous churches and organizations that I work with that are willing to systematically appropriate Apostolic Genius for the sake of the gospel in the West. You are the heroes at the frontline.

My shapevine.com buddies for being willing to innovate and pay the price.

The Warren family for taking the nomadic Hirsches into their lives.

Third Place Communities for being such fantastic guinea pigs.

Al and Lisa Dobson for adopting and embracing our beloved boxer Ruby.

Alan

Corry, my best friend, for giving me the space for projects like this.

The TPC crew for your companionship, commitment, and trust. The words I write and stories I tell are yours as well, forged from the years we've been together in mission.

Darryn

Special thanks to

Steve Ogne for adding to the content
and helping guide the outcomes.

Contents

Preface

As I write this preface, *The Forgotten Ways* has been out for around fifteen months. I can say that I have been genuinely humbled by the positive reception it has received. As an author I receive a lot of feedback through letters and e-mails or in person, and the nature of the feedback varies significantly. But by far the most common response I get from readers is, "I know this sounds strange, but I feel that I kind of 'remember' these ideas even though I have never been able to fully articulate them." At which point I usually say "hallelujah," because for me it is an affirmation of the whole idea behind *The Forgotten Ways*— that Apostolic Genius lies latent in all of God's people, and we have simply forgotten how to access it. We have become so numbed by the opiate of institutional religion that we have simply lost contact with the memory of what we can, and ought, to be. Another reason for my elation is that I believe the Spirit is indeed waking his people up to their hidden potential all across the world. The new emergence of apostolic movements is a global phenomenon, as far as I can tell, and it really is quite remarkable. We have cause for great hope.

But yet another response usually comes in the form of a question: "How can the ideas in *The Forgotten Ways* be implemented?" Most readers find themselves in organizations that feel worlds away from the *movement* ethos described in the book, even though they long to move in that direction. It is important to know that in writing *The Forgotten Ways* I never intended to develop a missional technique, but rather to awaken a lost imagination. We must go deep into our collective memories as God's people and "remember" the forgotten ways of apostolic movements. We need to think and dream and have our imaginations charged with possibilities and our hearts inspired by Jesus afresh. This workbook is not meant to short-circuit that much-needed recalibration, but rather to "operationalize" it.

To do this I needed some help. So I invited Darryn Altclass, a long-time friend and colleague, to write this book with me. Darryn is a dedicated and very savvy church planter who has consistently implemented much of the content of *The Forgotten Ways* into real-life practice over many years. He knows me well; we have worked closely together in Forge Mission Training Network and have shared many missional ideas and dreams together over the years. As a local movement pioneer, Darryn initiated Third Place Communities, which we use as the primary test case in the book. We have chosen this network not because of any supposed superiority, but simply because we have both traveled with it over the past few years as they have tried to integrate, with some degree of success, *The Forgotten Ways* into their common life.

We also received some needed guidance from friend and colleague Steve Ogne, an experienced trainer, coach, consultant, and author who works for CRM. Steve helped out with summarizing the information and was a faithful sounding board. We thank him for his insightful input along the way.

It's hard not to be perfectionistic about a book like this. I'm not sure if we would ever feel it fits the bill, but we offer it to you nonetheless. More importantly, we offer it to God in the hope that he might use it in the advancement of his kingdom in this critical century.

Sola Dei Gloria.

Alan Hirsch
May 2008

A Note to Leaders

The fact that you have begun to read this book indicates not only that you are interested in the theory of the forgotten ways, but that at some level you long to activate them in your own life and in the lives of those around you. This is exactly why we wrote this book.

This is not a theoretical book on mission or missional movements, although it does contain some theory. Rather, it's a practical handbook to provide frameworks and offer suggestions as a means to inspire God's people into mission. Our main purpose is to stir innovative missional action for Jesus in this post-Christian world we inhabit. More specifically, this handbook is a guide to the application of the ideas contained in *The Forgotten Ways*. We suggest you use it as a handbook, a kind of missional journal as you engage the world in mission. Make the book your own, use it well, take notes in the margins, underline, carry it with you, and jot down your ideas and reflections on the road.

Feedback suggests that many who have read *The Forgotten Ways* resonate deeply with the vision of the church articulated within the book. A lot of people reported they felt they were actually "remembering" something they had somehow forgotten, and that they gained a clearer insight into the life force (what Alan calls "Apostolic Genius") that pulsates through the early church and similar movements. We believe that the reason for this "remembering" is that Apostolic Genius actually resides in all authentic expressions of *ecclesia*, which has simply become dormant over time.

Many long to see something more akin to movements in the various churches and organizations to which they belong. However, they feel the reality of seeing that fulfilled is way beyond their grasp. Others who find themselves deeply embedded within various expressions of Christendom sense that it's an impossible task to transition their church into a missional movement.

Make no mistake; the scope of the change required to shift to the kind of movement described in *The Forgotten Ways* is nothing less than paradigmatic. Every element of mDNA (the name given to the components that together encode and form Apostolic Genius) poses a direct challenge to the prevailing ways of doing church and mission. When taken together, all six elements of Apostolic Genius might make the task seem somewhat overwhelming, but it is not as difficult as it seems, and certainly not impossible. The Chinese church proves that highly institutionalized forms of Christianity can actually become powerful transformative movements, given the right circumstances. And for the record, we don't believe we need persecution to activate Apostolic Genius. Less intense forms of adaptive challenges can, and do, force the church to respond. Because the church carries the gospel and by the power of the Spirit, the full coding of Apostolic Genius, the potential for world transformation is always present. God is able and very willing to empower the church to fulfill her missional calling. In fact, we see this as one of the very special works of the Holy Spirit—to awaken God's people to their calling and destiny as a movement that can and will change the world.

Akin to the idea of waking up to something long forgotten, we believe the church itself will "remember" the forgotten ways of apostolic movements. For this to happen, leaders will need to create the right environment and give meaningful vocabulary to what people are experiencing. This is precisely what we wish to achieve in writing this book—to make the forgotten ways, well . . . less forgotten.

Our hope is to help you, at whatever level (grassroots or strategic leadership), in whatever form of Christian organization, to reactivate the missional church *where you are*. We propose to do this by suggesting a set of habits and practices formed around each of the mDNA elements described in *The Forgotten Ways*. We believe this will allow us to "remember" once again what it means to be a transformative movement for Jesus in the West.

What's Inside?

Each chapter is structured in the same way, so that the users can expect some degree of uniformity. This approach basically comprises three sections.

1. A Summary of Each mDNA Element

This will provide the participant with an adequate overview of each chapter and mDNA element. It is relatively free of jargon, so it should be understandable by most. However, when somewhat technical phrases are retained, it will be the leader's task to explain them in a meaningful way. There is a glossary at the back of the book to help with this.

2. Suggested Habits and Practices

You will notice that after each summary we have arranged the practical section into Habits and Practices. Habits are the overall behavior we suggest groups adopt in order to appropriate the specific mDNA element, while practices are helpful ideas for living out the habits. The practices are simply proposed ways in which to act out or embody the habit in everyday life. Habits can be viewed as the framework of a ladder, and the practices as the rungs on which we place our feet.

Please note that these are suggested habits and practices. They are prompts, not prescriptions. Don't try doing them all; you will only exhaust yourself. In fact, you might not choose any of the ones we have suggested, but we hope that in that case, they might function simply as a stimulus for you to find your own.

3. A Group Learning Process

We wrote this book with a group context in mind. While people might choose to read the book in their own time, we recommend that the information is better processed with others. Our hope is that the information and examples contained within this book will prompt rich discussion and will lead groups into missional action. This is why we have called them action groups.

For this purpose you will find at the end of each chapter a set of questions for groups to use as a way to process and apply the principles. We believe that this is where great learning will occur as together you explore, evaluate, and begin to employ these concepts in community life. Here's an overview of the framework we suggest for group processing.

Session 1: Explore (talk about it)

In preparation please ensure everyone reads the chapter. Start with an overview of the mDNA element, to clarify the theme and associated concepts. If there are words or ideas people are not clear about, this is the time to clarify. It's a good idea for one person to take responsibility to guide this section, and for that person to have read (and understood) the associated chapter from *The Forgotten Ways*.

After the overview, explore the ideas and suggestions presented in the chapter. The exploration phase is highly relational and probes people's initial responses and feelings. Ask a few open-ended exploratory questions to allow the group space to share and think out loud. This is a good way to discern what's on the surface of people's minds and hearts and in need of discussion.

Session 2: Evaluate (reflect deeper)

While the exploration section encourages general sharing and relating, the evaluation phase is where deeper reflection and critical thinking occur. During this time ask questions and make statements that promote critical thinking. These questions will prompt the group to prioritize and brainstorm various options and alternatives. This is also where you identify blockages and resistance and sort out what is important and what is not.

Session 3: Employ (act on it)

The employing section is about moving the group into action. By this stage the group has explored the ideas through talking generally, evaluated by reflecting more deeply, identified barriers, and has begun to sort out what's important and what's not. Now it's time to probe the way ahead. What plan of action will the group employ as a way forward? This is where the group can start to refocus and respond by brainstorming and mapping out various options and action steps. What will they need to let go? What will they need to pick up? Who will they need help from? During this phase ask questions and make statements to provoke action.

Session 4: Personal Journal

After processing much information, we encourage you to take some time to pray, listen, and respond to God. How is God prompting you, and how will you respond? Take time to record your impressions as well as insights from the group. Write a prayer expressing your desires to God. If appropriate, share your thoughts in the group, and then pray together.

There are two other sections in the book, both found at the back.

Resource Section

We have included an appendix with relevant resources and examples that are referred to throughout the book. Due to the interrelated nature of Apostolic Genius, these resources are relevant to many different sections. That's why we've placed them together in a general resource section at the back. Just flick over to this section when needed or prompted.

Glossary

Because the primary book contains phrases and terms that might be obscure to many, we have included here the glossary (dictionary of terms used) from *The Forgotten Ways*. Feel free to read it first to familiarize yourself with some of these definitions. Rest assured, it will all become clearer as you go.

A Call to Action

To avoid the group becoming just another *discussion* group, we suggest you call them *action groups* or something to that effect. We don't want to foster mere understanding, but rather *informed* action. Whether you are using this book to guide a group of cell leaders or a small group trying to activate their cell, think of the handbook as a guide to the revolution, and of each member as an active participant in the movement. Remember that each and every Christian has the seed-potential for world transformation. Each can and must play a part. To embed a movement ethos throughout the church or organization, we suggest you recruit as many people as possible for the journey.

We recommend that someone assumes responsibility for coordinating the action group. The handbook is a standalone text, but it's very important that at least one person in the group has thoroughly read *The Forgotten Ways*, perhaps even twice, so that he or she can act as an informed guide along the journey. Leadership always necessitates a deeper appreciation of the issues. Whoever it is, this person should take responsibility at the beginning of each meeting to conduct the overview and to make sure everyone comprehends the basic ideas and terminology associated with Apostolic Genius. Alternatively, given that a great way to learn an idea is to actually teach it to others, you might like to suggest every member of the group takes a turn in teaching the overview. Given the complexity of the material at times, you might divide a chapter into two and distribute it to two different participants.

What follows is important information on how to get the most out of this handbook and maximize impact in your church and organization.

How to Apply the Apostolic Genius Model

There is no magic formula in using this handbook to apply the many ideas contained in *The Forgotten Ways*. Much will depend on both your context and the commitment of the group to search for the answers and then apply them in your situation. But we do suggest the following:

1. Get as Many to Read the Primary Text as Possible.

This is especially true for the key and influential leaders in the group. We recognize that *The Forgotten Ways* is a comprehensive text containing complex terminology and that it introduces many different paradigm shifts in how we think of church and movements. The reason for this comprehensiveness is to dislodge our thinking from the prevailing ideas and forms that seem to exercise a monopoly over our imaginations. We have so wedded our thinking of church to the institution that we no longer easily recognize a more dynamic Jesus movement when we see it. It is critical that we engage our minds and hearts in the quest to recover the forgotten ways of apostolic movements.

2. Get a Realistic Perspective on Change

Every group must deal with the issue of how long it will take to see Apostolic Genius genuinely embedded in the group or church. It is our clear belief that an established church can become significantly missional, but to do so the leaders will need to have a clear perspective on the change process needed to get this done. To a large degree this will depend on the situation of the organization when it starts the process. However, we are certain that to fully transform an existing organization will take significant time. However long you decide to take in study and applying the suggested practices, we encourage you to be patient, prayerful, and committed to sustain long-term change. Don't look for short-term solutions when the issues you deal with are complex. (You may want to read "A Crash Course in Chaos" in the addendum of *The Forgotten Ways* and try developing a change process along similar lines.[1])

3. Embed mDNA at the Core of the Organization/Church

In applying the Apostolic Genius model, it is essential to seek to implant mDNA at the very heart of the group. If you are a new church planter, then you have at least one advantage: you can clearly lay down the basic movemental approach and get it right from the start. If not a new church, then you will need to choose a strategic point of departure (see #5 below). Either way, to embed mDNA you will need to make sure that each member of your core team grapples with the ideas contained in *The Forgotten Ways* and begin to pre-empt how they might be integrated as you go. Much depends on what you build into the "stem cells" of the church. Corrupted DNA in any organism can cause mutations and problems later on, so don't be afraid to be a stickler about getting it right at the foundational level. But leaders will have to keep their eyes on things as they develop, because there is an innate tendency in all organizations to institutionalize over time. We have to assume that each member has most likely been deeply shaped by the institutional idea of church in its many forms. You will need to work hard to disembed the inherited imagination where it blocks the appropriation of Apostolic Genius (the combination of the six elements of mDNA).

4. Think Systems

The Forgotten Ways provides us with a system, a way of seeing movements in their wholeness. It is not a one-dimensional look at the simple characteristics of movements; rather, it describes the phenomenon of movements in their wholeness—as a system of interrelating and interconnected elements. The claim made in *The Forgotten Ways* is that the Apostolic Genius typology actually *applies to all Jesus movements that achieve hyperbolic growth*, or, as Roland Allen calls it, "spontaneous expansion." *The Forgotten Ways* is an attempt to describe the essential elements that come together and inform one another to create hyperbolic growth curves and high impact. Because the Apostolic Genius typology is a system, it is critical that you keep your eye on the whole while focusing on any of the singular elements. Never lose sight of the fact that a true apostolic movement needs all six elements to make it cook.

5. Use the Apostolic Genius Typology as a Strategic Tool

The user can adopt the Apostolic Genius typology to assess how close the organization is to being a genuine movement. It also can be used as a tool for strategic focus. For instance, taking the Apostolic Genius approach, you can assess the organization and identify the weakest elements. We suggest that the weakest element of mDNA then becomes the focus of strategic effort for that organization. Once that is developed over time, then the same process is undertaken to identify the next-weakest element, and that becomes the focus of effort until it is further developed, and so on. How do you do the assessment? If you can't develop your own, then there is a thoroughly researched online test available to help you in this regard. Go to www.theforgottenways .org, and you can take the mPULSE test there as regularly as you need to.[2]

6. *Resist Temptation to Use Any Single Element as a Silver Bullet*

Do not succumb to the temptation to treat any of the mDNA elements within itself as some sort of silver bullet, a quick cure for the ailments of your church. While developing one, say, discipleship, is likely to enhance the church, if you are seeking to engender apostolic movements, then none of the elements *by themselves* will be enough. Even though developing one will contribute to the whole system, it *takes all six to create an apostolic movement*. Each is necessary but not sufficient.

7. *Create Real-Life Action Heroes*

It is critical that you ensure that people are actually attempting to do what is being discussed and agreed upon. This is a handbook, and its task is not to stimulate conversations that lead nowhere, but to inspire and guide action. The real heroes of the group ought not to be the ones who can master the information intellectually, but rather those who are willing to give things a go and risk failure. You will need to inspire a culture of experimentation imbued with a genuine pioneering spirit.

8. *Be Realistic*

A word needs to be said about whether churches and organizations in Western contexts can become *exactly* like the movements described in *The Forgotten Ways*, namely the early church and the Chinese underground church. The straightforward answer is, probably not—at least not in the same way or to the same degree. There are many reasons for this. One is that we live in a post-Christian context that makes our task more complicated due to the inoculation of our culture against genuine expressions of Christianity. This is also due to the fact that we do not live in a premodern cultural context, but a postmodern one, where the structure of belief is far more complex. But this should not deter us from applying the Apostolic Genius model to our setting. Grassroots apostolic movements are definitely growing across the West, and in our opinion, they represent the hope and the future of Western Christianity. Not only is becoming a movement a challenge for most of us, but it is one that must be undertaken by as many churches and agencies as possible if we are to reestablish Christianity in the West. Failure here will mean the continuing decline of Christianity in every context in the West—and this is unacceptable to all committed to seeing the gospel appropriated and Jesus worshipped throughout our cities and neighborhoods.

As for the existing organization that finds itself largely bound to the institutional idea of church, this challenge should not be the cause of despair. Remember that every community that faithfully follows Jesus has all the latent potential already present within them. Our task is not to introduce faddish new ideas, but rather to awaken the collective memory and create the condition in which they can reactivate and reapply Apostolic Genius.

Our suggestion, therefore, is that you start using the strategic process suggested above and thus begin to *approximate* the kind of church expressed in apostolic movements. It is important to remember that in many ways, the churches and organizations we inhabit will to some degree always be hybrids—a mixture of organic and institutional elements. The challenge for most of us will be to continually move toward being more movemental by increasingly applying the Apostolic Genius typology with its six elements. It is our contention that at a certain catalytic moment, when the six elements are present and interacting in a significant way, spontaneous expansion *will* begin to occur.

Rationale for the Handbook

Two interrelated educational philosophies guided the formation of this handbook. First, given our current state of knowledge and how we gain it, we have to shift from trying to *think our way into a new way of acting* to the process of *acting our way into a new way of thinking*. The other guiding concept is related to action (praxis) as a basis of insight into God, discipleship, and church. There is a fundamental difference between core values and core practices.

Acting Our Way into a New Way of Thinking

We are all familiar with the gospel story in which Jesus selected a band of disciples, lived and ministered with them, and mentored them on the road. It was this life-on-life phenomenon that facilitated the transfer of information and ideas into concrete situations. The idea of discipleship will be explored in one of the chapters; we simply note that this is the way Jesus formed his disciples and that we should not think we could generate authentic disciples in any other way.

Please don't misunderstand us; we do need serious intellectual engagement with the key ideas of our time, but what is truly concerning is that such engagement largely takes place in the disengaged and passive environment of the classroom. This is simply not the way Jesus taught us to develop disciples. And it is not that Jesus lacked an appropriate model of the classroom—the Greeks had developed this hundreds of years before Christ, and it was well entrenched in the Greco-Roman world. The Hebrew worldview was a life-oriented one and was not primarily concerned with concepts and ideas *in themselves*. We simply do not believe that we can continue to try and *think* our way into a new way of acting; but rather, we need to *act* our way into new way of thinking.[3]

How did we move so far from the ethos of discipleship passed on to us by our Lord? The cause lies in Western Christianity being so deeply influenced by Greek, or Hellenistic, ideas of knowledge. By the fourth century, in the church the Platonic worldview had almost triumphed over the Hebraic one. Later, it was Aristotle who became the predominant philosopher for the church. He too operated under a Hellenistic framework. Essentially a Hellenistic view of knowledge is concerned about concepts, ideas, and the nature of being. The Hebraic on the other hand, is primarily concerned with issues of concrete existence, obedience, life-oriented wisdom, and interrelationship of all things under God. As Jews, Jesus and the early church quite clearly operated primarily out of a Hebraic understanding rather than a Hellenistic one.

The diagram below demonstrates this distinction. If our starting point is *old thinking* and *old behavior*, and we see it as our task to change that situation, taking the Hellenistic approach will mean that we provide information to try and get the person or church to a new way of thinking—and hopefully to a new way of acting. The problem is that by merely addressing intellectual aspects we have failed to be able to change behavior. The assumption in Hellenistic thinking is that if people get the right ideas, they will simply change their behavior. The

Hellenistic approach therefore can be characterized as an attempt to try and *think our way into a new way of acting*. Both experience and history show the fallacy of this approach. And it certainly does not make disciples. All we do is change the way a person *thinks*, and their behavior remains largely unaffected. Even though gaining knowledge is essential to transformation, we soon discover that it's going to take a whole lot more than new thinking to transform us.

So what is that better way? We mentioned it before. It's found in the ancient art of disciple making, which operates best with the Hebrew understanding of knowledge. We need to take the whole person into account in seeking to transform an individual, and educate them in the context *of* life *for* life. The way we do this, is the way Jesus did it, *to act our way into a new way of thinking*. So whether we find ourselves with old thinking and old behavior, or new thinking and old behavior, the way forward is to put actions into the equation.

The assumption is that we bring all these dynamic thinking processes with us into our actions. It is all about context, not just content. We do not, as is supposed by the Hellenistic model, leave our thinking behind when we are doing our actions. We think while we are acting, and act while we our thinking. So what we are proposing looks something like this. . . .

Figure 1
Action-Learning (Discipleship) vs. the Academy

At Forge Mission Training Network, we have built the entire system around this concept of action-learning discipleship. Our twin aims are to develop missionaries to the West, along with a distinct pioneering missional mode of leadership. To do this, we host an internship where each intern is placed in an environment of mission. The vast majority of the intern's learning is by "having a go" in mission. They also meet regularly with a coach for reflection and goal setting, and attend inspiring intensives where they are exposed to a significant amount of theory. This information is communicated by those who have a demonstrated capacity to model what they are teaching—in other words, they are active practitioners in their own right. Engaging in training in this way, the intern's ability to grasp the issues, to resolve and integrate them, is significantly increased.

Core Practices vs. Core Values

Closely related to the idea of action-learning described above, is the distinction between core values and core practices. Keep this distinction in mind, because the content of this book is structured around the idea of developing *core practices* as a means of changing church culture.

Following standard business practice, many churches use the idea of developing core values to help shape organizational culture. The core values, along with vision and mission statements, are created to guide the organization's activities and shape its culture. The weakness of this approach is that they can easily become mere "motherhood statements," preferred rather than actual values. If you don't develop practices based on the values, establishing core values simply becomes an intellectual process rather than informing behavior. It is very hard to change people's values by referring them to a new set of values on paper that they're meant to believe in and assimilate into their lives. So we suggest focusing your efforts on a raft of possible practices, which if applied, will inform behavior and so change thinking as a result.

We will suggest this again later, but the process of moving from values to practices can be developed in the following way. Identify the core value you wish to integrate, and state it clearly. Once the idea is clear, work together to ask the question, "What action, if applied, will most consistently *embody* this core value in the organization?" It's important to seek to link the action as closely as possible to the ordinary rhythms in life. For example, if a core value of the group is hospitality, don't just say, "We value hospitality." Rather, look for natural ways in which the community might actually practice hospitality.

Calling for a Conspiracy of Little Jesuses

The instinct, power, and genius of the early church rests within the memory of God's people, and so we call for pioneering mission-hearted groups to stir that memory into action. We honestly believe that the hope of Western Christianity rests within each group of Christians living out their calling to be God's people in the localities where they work, rest, and play.

If we're going to impact our world in the name of Jesus, it will be because people like you and me took action in the power of the Spirit. Ever since the mission and ministry of Jesus, God has never stopped calling for a movement of "Little Jesuses" to follow him into the world and unleash the remarkable redemptive genius that lies in the very message we carry. Given the situation of the church in the West, much will now depend on whether we are willing to break out of a stifling herd instinct and find God again in the context of the advancing kingdom of God.

"Whatever you can do, or dream you can, begin it.
Boldness has genius, power and magic in it."

—attributed to Johann Wolfgang Goethe

1

Introduction to *The Forgotten Ways*

After a time of decay comes the turning point. The powerful light that has been banished returns. There is movement, but it is not brought about by force. . . . the movement is natural, arising spontaneously. The old is discarded and the new is introduced. Both measures accord with the time; therefore no harm results."

—*I Ching*

Before delving into the details of practicing the forgotten ways, it's important to take an overview of the core ideas. Some of you will have read the original text, and others will have not. Either way it will be helpful to be familiar with the key information. For this purpose simply insert the original introduction here as a point of entry for those who haven't read the book and as a refresher for those that have read it. It goes like this . . .

Imagine there was a power which lies hidden at the very heart of God's people. Suppose this power was built into the initiating 'stem cell' of the church by the Holy Spirit but was buried and lost through centuries of neglect and disuse. Imagine that if rediscovered, this hidden power could unleash remarkable energies that could propel Christianity well into the twenty-second century. Is this not something that we who love God and his cause would give just about anything to recover? The idea of latent inbuilt missional potencies is not a mere fantasy; in fact there are primal forces that lie latent in every Jesus community and in every true believer. Not only does such a thing exist but it is a clearly identifiable phenomenon that has energized history's most outstanding Jesus movements, perhaps the most remarkable expression of which is very much with us today. This extraordinary power is being recovered in certain expressions of Western Christianity, but not without significant challenge to, and resistance from, the current way in which we do things.

The fact that you have started reading this book will mean that not only are you interested in the search for a more authentic expression of *ecclesia* (the NT word for church), but you are in some sense aware of the dramatic changes in worldview that have been taking place in general culture over the last fifty years. Whatever one may call it, this shift from the modern to the postmodern, or from solid modernity to liquid modernity, has generally been difficult for the church to accept. We find ourselves lost in a perplexing global jungle where our well used cultural and theological maps don't seem to fit. It seems we have woken up to find ourselves in contact with a strange and unexpected reality that seems to defy our usual ways of dealing with issues of the church and its mission. All this amounts to a kind of ecclesial future-shock where we are left wandering in a world we can no longer recognize. In the struggle to grasp our new reality, churches and church leaders have become painfully aware that our inherited concepts, our language, indeed our whole way of thinking are inadequate to describe what is going on both in and around us. The problems raised in such a situation are not merely intellectual ones but together amount to an intense spiritual, emotional, and existential crisis.

The truth is that the twenty-first century is turning out to be a highly complex phenomenon where terrorism, technological innovation, an unsustainable environment, rampant consumerism, and discontinuous change confront us at every point. In the face of this, even the most confident among us in our more honest moments would have to admit that the church as we know it faces a very significant adaptive challenge. The overwhelming majority of church leadership today report that they feel it is getting much harder for their communities to negotiate the complexities before them. And as a result the church is on massive, long-trended, decline in the West. In this situation, we have to ask ourselves probing questions, "Will more of the same do the trick? Do we have the inherited resources to deal with this situation? Can we simply rework the tried and true Christendom understanding of church which we so love and understand, and finally, in an ultimate tweak of the system, come up with the winning formula?" [1]

If we are honest, it seems that the inherited formulas simply won't work anymore. And there are many others who think this way. There is a massive roaming of the mind going on in our day as the search for alternatives heats up. However, most of the new thinking as it relates to the future of Christianity in the West only highlights our dilemma and generally proposes solutions that are little more than revisions of past approaches and techniques. Even much of the thinking about the so-called Emerging Church leaves the prevailing assumptions of church and mission intact and simply focuses on the issue of theology and spirituality in a post-modern setting. This amounts to reworking the theological "software" whilst ignoring the "hardware" as well as "operating system" of the church. In my opinion this will not be enough to get us through. As we anxiously gaze into the future and delve back into our history and traditions to retrieve missiological tools from the Christendom toolbox, many of us are left with the sinking feeling that this is simply not going to work. The tools and techniques that fitted previous eras of Western history simply don't seem to work any longer. What we need now is a new set of tools. A new "paradigm"—a new vision of reality: a fundamental change in our thoughts, perceptions, and values, especially as they relate to our view of the church and mission.

And it's not that reaching into our past is not part of the solution. It is. The issue is that we generally don't go back far enough; or rather, that we don't delve *deep* enough for our answers. Every now and again we do get glimpses of an answer, but because of the radical and disturbing nature of the remedy we retreat to the safety of the familiar and the controllable. The *real* answers, if we have the courage to search for and apply them, are usually more radical than we are normally given to think, and because of this they undermine our sense of place in the world with its status quo—not something that the Western church has generally been too comfortable with. But we are now living in a time when only a solution that goes to the very roots of what it means to be Jesus' people will do.

The conditions facing us in the twenty-first century not only pose a threat to our existence but also present us with an extraordinary opportunity to discover ourselves in a way that orients us to this complex challenge in ways that are resonant with an ancient energy. This energy not only links us with the powerful impulses of the original church, but also gives us wings with which to fly. *The Forgotten Ways* primary text could be labeled under the somewhat technical category of *missional ecclesiology*, because it explores the nature of the Christian movements, and the church as it is shaped by Jesus and his mission. But don't be fooled by the drab terminology—missional ecclesiology is dynamite. Mainly because the church (the *ecclesia*), when true to its calling, and on about what God is on about, is by far the most potent force for transformational change the world has seen. *The Forgotten Ways* was written in the hope that the church in the West can, by the power of the Holy Spirit, arouse and reengage that amazing power that lies within us.

A Journey of a Thousand Miles Begins with a Single Question

In 2003 I attended a seminar on missional church where the speaker asked a question. "How many Christians do you think there were in the year AD 100?" He then asked, "How many Christians do you think there were just before Constantine came on the scene, say, AD 310?"[2] Here is the somewhat surprising answer.

100 AD	As few as 25,000 Christians
310 AD	Up to 20,000,000 Christians

He then asked the question which has haunted me to this day, "How did they do this?" "How did they grow from being a small movement to the most significant religious force in the Roman Empire in two centuries?" Now *that's* a question to initiate a journey! And delving into this question drove me to the discovery of what I will call Apostolic Genius—the inbuilt life force and guiding mechanism of God's people—and the living components or elements that make it up. These components I have tagged missional DNA or mDNA for short.

So let me ask *you* the question—how *did* the early Christians do it? And before you respond, here are some qualifications you must factor into your answer.

- *They were an illegal religion throughout this period*: At best, they were tolerated; at the very worst they were very severely persecuted.
- *They didn't have any church buildings as we know them*: While archaeologists have discovered chapels dating from this period, they were definite exceptions to the rule and they tended to be very small converted houses.
- *They didn't even have the Scriptures as we know them*: They were putting the canon together during this period.
- *They didn't have an institution or the professional form of leadership normally associated with it*. At times of relative calm, prototypical elements of institution did appear, but by what we consider institutional, these were at best pre-institutional.
- *They didn't have seeker sensitive services, youth groups, worship bands, seminaries, or commentaries, etc.*
- *They actually made it hard to join the church*. By the late second century aspiring converts had to undergo a significant initiation period to prove they were worthy.

In fact they had none of the things we would ordinarily employ to solve the problems of the church, and yet they grew from twenty five thousand to twenty million in two hundred years! *So, how did the early church do it?* In answering that question, we can perhaps find the answer to the question for the church and mission in our day and in our context. For herein lies the powerful mystery of church in its most authentic form.

But before the example of the Early Christian Movement can be dismissed as a freak of history, there is another perhaps even more astounding manifestation of Apostolic Genius,[3] that unique and explosive power inherent in all of God's people, in our own time—namely, the underground church in China. Theirs is a truly remarkable story: About the time when Mao Zedong took power and initiated the systemic purge of religion from society, the church in China which was well established and largely modeled on Western forms due to colonization, was estimated to number about two million adherents. As part of the this systematic persecution, Mao banished all foreign missionaries and ministers, nationalized all church property, killed all the senior leaders, either killed or imprisoned all second and third level leaders, banned all public meetings of Christians with the threat of death or torture, and then proceeded to perpetrate one of the cruelest persecutions of Christians on historical record.

The explicit aim of the Cultural Revolution was to obliterate Christianity (and all religion) from China. At the end of the reign of Mao and his system in the late 70's, and the subsequent lifting of the so-called Bamboo Curtain in the early 80's, foreign missionaries and church officials were allowed back into the country, albeit under strict supervision. They expected to find the church decimated and the disciples a weak and battered people. On the contrary, they discovered that Christianity had flourished beyond all imagination. The estimates *then* were about 60 million Christians in China, and counting! And it has grown significantly since then. David Aikman, former Beijing bureau chief for *Time* magazine, suggests in his book *Jesus in Beijing* that Christians may number as many as 80 million.[4] If anything, in the Chinese phenomenon, we are witnessing the most significant transformational Christian movement in the history of the church. And remember, not unlike the early church these people had very few Bibles (at times they shared only one page to a house church and then swapped that page with another house group.) They had no professional clergy, no official leadership structures, no central organization, no mass meetings, and yet they grew like mad. How is this possible? How did they do it?[5]

But we can observe similar growth patterns in other historical movements. Steve Addison[6] notes that by the end of John Wesley's lifetime one in thirty English men and women had become Methodists. In 1776 less than 2 percent of Americans were Methodists. By 1850, the movement claimed the allegiance of 34 percent of the population. How did they do it?

These are dangerous stories because they subvert us into a journey that will call us to more radical expression of Christianity than the one we currently experience. It was the central task of The Forgotten Ways to give a name to these phenomena and attempt to identify the elements which constitute it. The phenomenon present in these dangerous stories I call Apostolic Genius and the elements that make it up I have named mDNA. They will be defined fully later. The object of The Forgotten Ways is to explore Apostolic Genius and try to interpret it for our own missional context and situation in the West. These two key examples (the Early Church and the Chinese Church) have been chosen not only because they are truly remarkable movements, but also because one is ancient and the other contemporary and so we can observe Apostolic Genius in two radically different contexts. I have also chosen them because both movements faced significant threats to their survival; in both cases this took the form of systematic persecution. This is significant because as will be explained later, the church in the West faces its own form of adaptive challenge as we negotiate the complexities of the twenty-first century—one that threatens our very survival.

Persecution drove both the early Christian movement and the Chinese church to discover their truest nature as an apostolic people. Persecution forced them away from any possible reliance on any form of centralized religious institution and caused them to live closer to, and more consistently with, their primal message, namely the gospel. We have to assume that if one is willing to die for being a follower of Jesus then in all likelihood that person is a real believer. This persecution, under the sovereignty of God, acted as a means to keep these movements true to their faith and reliant on God—it purified them from the dross and any other unnecessary churchly paraphernalia. It was by *being true to* the gospel that they unleashed the power of Apostolic Genius. And this is a huge lesson for us: as we face our own challenges we will need to be sure about our faith and who it is in whom we trust or else risk the eventual demise of Christianity as a religious force in Western history—witness Europe in the last hundred years.

In pursuit of the answer to *that question*, the question of how these phenomenal Jesus movements actually did it, I have become convinced that the power that manifested itself in the dangerous stories of these two remarkable movements, is available to us as well. And the awakening of that dormant potential has something to do with the strange mixture of the passionate love of God, prayer, and incarnational practice. Add to this mix, appropriate modes of leadership (as expressed in Ephesians 4), the recovery of radical discipleship, relevant forms of organization and structures, and the suitable conditions for these to be able to catalyze. When these factors come together, the situation is ripe for something remarkable to take place.

To nail down this rather elusive concept of dormant (or latent) potentials, recall the story of *The Wizard of Oz*. The central character in this well-loved movie is Dorothy, who was transported in a tornado from Kansas to the magical Land of Oz. Wanting to return home, she gets guidance from Glinda, the Good Witch of the North, who advises her to walk to the Emerald City and there consult the Wizard. On the yellow brick road she acquires three companions: the Scarecrow, who hopes the Wizard will be able to give him some brains; the Tin Woodsman, who wants the Wizard to give him a heart; and the Lion, who hopes to obtain courage. After surviving some dangerous encounters with the Wicked Witch of the West and numerous other nasty creatures, they eventually make it to see the Wizard, only to find out he is a hoax. They leave the Emerald City brokenhearted. But the Wicked Witch, perceiving the magic in Dorothy's ruby slippers, won't leave them alone. After a final encounter with the Wicked Witch and her minions, they overcome the source of evil and thereby liberate Oz. But through all their ordeals and in their final victory they discover that in fact they already have what they were looking for—in fact they had it all along. The Scarecrow is very clever, the Tinman has real heart, and the Lion turns out to be very brave and courageous after all. They didn't need the Wizard at all. What they needed was a situation that forced them to discover, or activate that which was already in them. They had what they were looking for, only they didn't realize it. To cap it off, Dorothy had her answer to her wish all along; she had the capacity to return home to Kansas—in her ruby slippers. By clicking them together three times, she is transported back to her home in Kansas.

This story highlights the central assumption here and gives a hint to why it has been called *The Forgotten Ways*: namely, that all God's people carry within themselves the same potencies that energized the early Christian movement and the Chinese church. Apostolic Genius lies dormant in you, me, and every local church that seeks to follow Jesus faithfully in any time. We have quite simply forgotten how to access and trigger it.

A Sneak Preview

Here is where the rubber hits the road. Here is the heart of the book as it attempts to describe Apostolic Genius and the constituent elements of mDNA that make it blaze up. Einstein said that when the solution is simple, God is speaking. Following this advice, I have tried to discern quintessential elements that combine to create Apostolic Genius and to simplify them to the absolutely irreducible components. There are six simple but interrelating elements of mDNA, forming a complex and living structure. These present us with a powerful paradigm grid with which we will be able to assess our current understandings and experiences of church and mission. They are:

- **Jesus Is Lord:** At the center and circumference of every significant Jesus movement resides a very simple confession. Simple, but one that fully vibrates with the primal energies of the scriptural faith, namely, the claim of One God over every aspect of every life, and the response of his people to that claim (Deut. 6:4–6ff). The way that this was expressed in the New Testament and later movements was simply "Jesus Is Lord!" With this simple confession they changed the world.
- **Disciple Making:** Essentially this involves the irreplaceable, and lifelong, task of becoming like Jesus by embodying his message. This is perhaps where many of our efforts fail. Disciple-making is an irreplaceable core task of the church and needs to be structured into every church's basic formula.
- **Missional-Incarnational Impulse**: This refers to the twin impulses of remarkable missional movements. Namely the dynamic outward thrust and the related deepening impulse which together *seed* and *embed* the gospel into different cultures and people groups.
- **Apostolic Environment**: This refers to apostolic influence and the fertile environment it creates in initiating and maintaining the phenomenal movements of God. This will relate to the type of leadership and ministry required to sustain metabolic growth.
- **Organic Systems**: This relates to the idea of appropriate structures for metabolic growth. Phenomenal Jesus movements grow precisely because they do not have centralized institutions to block

growth through control. Here we will find that remarkable Jesus movements have the feel of a movement, structure as a network, and spread like viruses.

- *Communitas*, not **Community**: The most vigorous forms of community are those that come together in the context of a shared ordeal. Communitas emerges from communities who define themselves as a group with a mission that lies beyond them, thus initiating a risky journey. Everyone loves an adventure. Or do we?

Apostolic Genius is the phrase I developed to try to name the unique energy and force that pulsates through the remarkable Jesus movements in history. My own conclusions are that Apostolic Genius is made up of six components, or elements, called mDNA. These six elements are briefly described above. Loaded into the term Apostolic Genius is the full combination of all the elements of mDNA that together form a system, as it were, each informing and impacting the other. As already stated, Apostolic Genius is latent, or embedded, into the very nature of God's gospel people. I suggest that when all the elements of mDNA are present and are in dynamic relationship with the other elements, and an adaptive challenge acts as a catalyst, then Apostolic Genius is activated.

And so the system of Apostolic Genius will look something like this. . . .

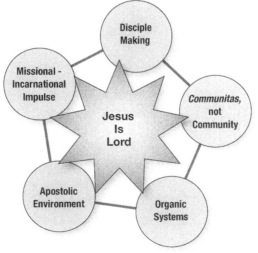

Figure 2
The Structure of Apostolic Genius

Suffice to say here that in exploring these ideas I feel that I am peering into things that are very deep, things that, if recovered and applied, could have considerable ramifications for Western Christianity. I say this as someone who is not claiming something as my own. If anything, like all who receive a grace from God, I feel that I am the humble recipient of a revelation, an unearthing of something primal, in which I am privileged to participate. *The Forgotten Ways* is a stumbling attempt to articulate that ever elusive revelation of the nature of Apostolic Genius—something that belongs to the gospel itself and therefore to the whole people who live by it. Albert Einstein said that when he was peering into the mysteries of the atom he felt he was peering over God's shoulder into things remarkable and wonderful. I must admit to feeling the same sense of awe as I look into these things.

2

The Heart of It All

Jesus Is Lord

When Paul completes his exploration into the mystery of God's involvement in our world, he soars into an ecstatic doxology: "Oh, the depth of the riches of the wisdom and knowledge of God! How unsearchable his judgments, and his paths beyond tracing out! 'Who has known the mind of the Lord? Or who has been his counselor?' 'Who has ever given to God, that God should repay him?' For from him and through him and to him are all things. To him be the glory forever! Amen" (Rom. 11:33–36). The clarity of truth dawns upon Paul in utter simplicity, and through these timeless words he points us to the very core of a Hebraic understanding of God: "for from him and through him and to him are all things." Here we touch the epicenter of the biblical consciousness of God to which we must return if we are to renew the church in our day.

It is hard to determine where to place material that by its very nature is more than just an "element" of Apostolic Genius. All genuine Christian movements involve at their spiritual core an encounter with the One True God. If we fail to apprehend this spiritual center of the Jesus movements, we can never fully understand them, nor can we invoke the power that infused their lives and communities. While in some sense this is an element of Apostolic Genius, it is actually much more than that. This consciousness of God pervades the entire phenomenon.

Distilling the Message

Most people, when asked about how they think these remarkable movements grew so amazingly, answer that it was because they were true believers. That is, there was an authenticity to their faith and they were obviously empowered by the Holy Spirit. Any study of the lives of these people cannot fail to inspire. In the context of persecution, they lived very close to their message. They clung to the gospel and unlocked its liberating power. They jettisoned all unnecessary clutter and theological paraphernalia and distilled the message to its essence. Under these conditions, faith was once again linked in utter simplicity to Jesus. The gospel became a possession of the people—profoundly grassroots, easy to get, and simple to pass on. These movements "traveled light," and in the process discovered their true message. At the heart of all great movements is a recovery of a simple Christology—in a very literal sense, they are *Jesus* movements.

This phenomenon of a movement identifying, distilling, and living by its message is a massive clue to Apostolic Genius and how we can recover it in the West. But in order to distill the message, we need to return to the primary theme of the Bible: God's redemptive claim over our lives.

Hear, O Israel

So what was this uncluttered message distilled by these remarkable movements? A study of these groups shows the answer is found in biblical monotheism—an encounter with the One God who claims and saves us. When the Early Christians confess that "Jesus is Lord," it wasn't a simple affirmation that Jesus is our Master and we his servants. It

certainly is that, but given the Hebraic context, the confession relates
back to Israel's primary declaration, "*Yahweh is Lord*." It touches the
deepest currents in biblical revelation that take us directly to the nature
of God, his relation to his world, and his claim over every aspect of
our lives. It all starts with Israel's basic confession, the *Shema Yisrael*
(Hear, O Israel) based on Deuteronomy 6:4.

To truly appreciate the power of this claim we need to set it in its
original context—that of religious pluralism or polytheism. People
living in the ancient Near East were deeply spiritual and recognized
that life was filled with the sacred, the mystical, and the magical. There
were numerous gods who were seen to rule over every different sphere
of life. There was a god of the field, a god of the forest, a god of the
river, of politics, of family, of fertility, and so on. The simple action
of going to the river to draw water via the field and through the forest
was actually quite complex. Every god must be appeased. And into this
environment comes the *Shema* . . .

> Hear, O Israel: The LORD our God, the LORD is one. Love the LORD
> your God with all your heart and with all your soul and with all your
> strength. These commandments that I give you today are to be upon
> your hearts. Impress them on your children. Talk about them when you
> sit at home and when you walk along the road, when you lie down and
> when you get up. Tie them as symbols on your hands and bind them on
> your foreheads. Write them on the doorframes of your houses and on
> your gates. (Deut. 6:4–9)

This declaration has direct and far-reaching implications. No longer
could there be different gods for the various spheres of life. Yahweh is
the ONE God who rules over every aspect of life. Yahweh is Lord of
home, field, politics, work, etc., and the religious task was to honor
this ONE God in and through all aspects of life. It was a call for the
Israelite to live his or her life under the lordship of one God and not
under the tyranny of the many gods. So in the Hebraic perspective,
monotheism is not so much a statement about God in his oneness
as it is a claim that there is only one God and he is Lord of all. This
"practical monotheism" lies at the epicenter of Israel's, and therefore
the biblical concept, of faith. God is concerned with every aspect of
the believer's life, not just the so-called spiritual dimensions. There

is no such thing as sacred and secular in a biblical worldview. It can conceive of no part of the world that does not come under the claim of Yahweh's lordship. All of life belongs to God, and true holiness means bringing all the spheres under God. This is what constitutes biblical worship.

Jesus Is Lord

The incarnation does not alter the fundamental practical monotheism of the scriptures; rather, it restructures it around Jesus Christ. He becomes the focal point in our relationship to God. Jesus not only initiates the new covenant; he *is* the New Covenant. "Jesus is Lord" is the covenant claim of God over our lives—the unshakable center of the Christian creed and confession. When the early church claims "Jesus is Lord," it does so in precisely the same way, and with exactly the same implications that Israel claimed God as Lord in the *Shema*. Our spiritual forebears really understood the inner meaning of monotheism. They knew that Jesus was Lord and that this lordship effectively excluded all other claims to loyalty. They knew that this was the heart of the faith, and they could not, would not, surrender it.

The Heart of Things

At its very heart, Christianity is a messianic movement, one that seeks to consistently embody the life, spirituality, and mission of its Founder. We have made it so many other things, but this is its utter simplicity. Discipleship, becoming like Jesus our Lord and Founder, lies at the epicenter of the church's task. In order to recover the ethos of authentic Christianity, we need to refocus our attention back to the Root and recalibrate ourselves around Jesus.

A genuinely messianic monotheism therefore breaks down any notions of a false separation between the "sacred" and the "secular." If the world and all in it belongs to God, then there can be no sphere of life that is not open to the rule of God. There can be no non-God area in our lives or culture. Consider the following diagrams. The first illustrates a dualistic approach; the second offers an alternative.

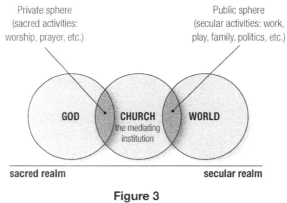

Private sphere
(sacred activities:
worship, prayer, etc.)

Public sphere
(secular activities: work,
play, family, politics, etc.)

GOD   CHURCH   WORLD
the mediating
institution

sacred realm   secular realm

Figure 3
Dualistic Spirituality

Now, using the same elements and realigning them to fit a nondu-alistic understanding of God, church, and world, we can reconfigure this as follows:

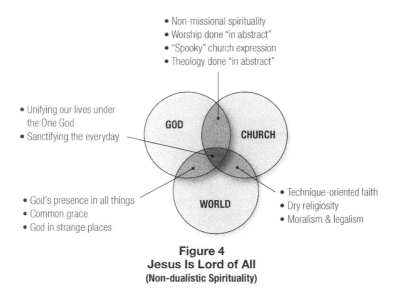

- Non-missional spirituality
- Worship done "in abstract"
- "Spooky" church expression
- Theology done "in abstract"

- Unifying our lives under
  the One God
- Sanctifying the everyday

GOD   CHURCH

- God's presence in all things
- Common grace
- God in strange places

WORLD

- Technique-oriented faith
- Dry religiosity
- Moralism & legalism

Figure 4
Jesus Is Lord of All
(Non-dualistic Spirituality)

Seeing things this way leads us to embrace an all-of-life perspective to our faith. By refusing the false dualism of sacred or secular, and by committing all of our lives under Jesus, we live out true holiness. There is nothing in our lives that should not and cannot be brought under the rule of God. If we fail to do this, then while we might be *confessing monotheists*, we might end up *practicing polytheists*. Dualistic expressions of faith always result in practical polytheism. Christ-centered monotheism demands loyalty precisely where the other gods claim it. Make no mistake, we are surrounded by the claims of false gods who clamor for our loyalties—not the least of these the worship of wealth and the associated gods of consumerism.

Sadly, history demonstrates how we as God's people can so often obscure the centrality of Jesus in our experience of church. There is so much clutter in our "religion" that this central unifying claim that lies at the heart of the faith is easily lost. It is remarkable how Jesus can be so easily cast out from among his people. Have you ever wondered why in Revelation 3:20 Jesus is seen standing outside his church, knocking at the door and asking to come in? How did he get out from among his people in the first place?

This section has sought to identify the epicenter of mDNA and therefore a critical element of Apostolic Genius. The other elements in the structure of mDNA form themselves around and are guided by it. The confession "Jesus is Lord" is a challenge to take seriously the absolute and ongoing centrality of Jesus for Christianity as a movement and for each local gathering. As we have seen, the early Christian movement and the Chinese underground church discovered this as their sustaining and guiding center in the midst of a massive adaptive challenge. No less is required of us as we seek to negotiate the challenge of the twenty-first century. The first step in the revival of Apostolic Genius is the recovery of the lordship of Jesus in its utter simplicity.

Now we'd like to suggest a few habits and practices that promote Jesus as Lord among us.

Suggested Habits and Practices

In order to recover the heart of Apostolic Genius, we must learn to recalibrate every part of our lives around Jesus. So what does this mean practically for those seeking to become an influential movement in the West? Here are a few suggestions.

1. Keep Jesus at the heart of it all
2. Get over dualism
3. Make the Gospels the primary text

Habit 1: Keep Jesus at the Heart of It All

In the remarkable Jesus movements, at the heart of it all the followers' faith was linked in utter simplicity to Jesus. They shed all unnecessary clutter, embraced a simple Christology, and in the process grew into a grassroots Jesus movement. For them, Jesus was *the heart of it all*, and they worked hard to keep it that way. Some even died for it. At the very core, Christianity is not a religion but a Jesus-fueled movement that seeks to consistently embody the life, spirituality, and mission of its Founder.

Practice One: Seek a Fresh Perspective on Jesus

The first practice we suggest in keeping Jesus at the heart of it all is to seek a fresh perspective on his life and mission. Our particular institutional perspectives and belief systems, with all their trappings, have the potential to cloud the core truths of Christ and his gospel. Over time it's relatively easy to lose sight of the fundamentals and become caught up in a myriad of other *secondary* causes. In this case, it's helpful to bypass all the historical culture and start afresh. We need to take a fresh look at the central person of the faith and return to the unencumbered Christology of the New Testament Church.

- The first followers would have understood Jesus and his teaching primarily through Jewish eyes. To understand Jesus correctly, it's helpful to comprehend Jesus's heritage and the context in which he lived and ministered. From here we can construct a fresh and vibrant Christology.
- Read up on a Jewish perspective of faith. A great place to start is chapter 7, "The God of Israel and the Renewal of Christianity," in Alan's book *The Shaping of Things to Come*.[1] There you will find a helpful overview of looking at Jesus through Hebraic eyes.
- In studying the context in which Jesus lived and ministered, you might like to explore books as a community such as *ReJesus* by Alan Hirsch and Michael Frost,[2] *The Jesus I Never Knew* by Philip Yancey,[3] or *The Divine Conspiracy* by Dallas Willard.[4] Other texts, such as *Poet & Peasant* and *Through Peasant Eyes* by Kenneth E. Bailey,[5] are classics. Working through Stanley Hauerwas's fantastic

commentary on Matthew would be a great exercise.[6] All of N. T. Wright's material on Jesus is extremely helpful as well.[7]

- Adopt a standard text that everyone in the community is encouraged to read in the first year. You could also make reading a core text on Christology part of the formation process into the faith community.
- Distill your core message to a simple Christology. If you insist on having a written theological statement, ensure it is secondary and points to a clear understanding of Jesus and what he is to us. Try to avoid making things too complex.
- Watch movies on the life of Jesus; then reflect on them together. Discuss their strengths and weaknesses and their relationship to the Gospel accounts.
- To become familiar with the ways of God in Jesus, read and reread the Gospels (see the habit "Make the Gospels the Primary Text," below).

Practice Two: Shape Life and Spirituality on Jesus

The second practice we suggest is to pattern our individual and collective spiritualities on Jesus. He is our model and primary reference point for all genuine expressions of spirituality. The golden questions are, "What did Jesus's spirituality look like and consist of?" and "How does our spirituality compare?" Reflecting on these two questions is a good place to start.

- As a group, research the spirituality of Jesus, and gather your findings under a few headings. Then, using this as a template, evaluate your own personal and collective spirituality. How do you think you will measure up? Do you imagine you'll go close to matching up? Taking one area at a time, brainstorm ways to shape a more Jesus-centered spirituality across your community.
- Jesus modeled a radical spirituality of engagement with the world. He was known as a friend of sinners. His spirituality was intriguing and magnetic. He ate and drank with prostitutes as well as the religious elite. He touched lepers and socialized with tax collectors and women. In fact his spirituality got him into a lot of

trouble with both the religious and civil authorities of the day. What are you and your community known for? Could these same characterizations apply? Why don't you ask those around you? That would be a telling exercise!

- Here's another exercise to reset your communal life on Jesus. As a faith community, evaluate everything you do—all your programs, gatherings, ministries, and so on. Ask whether you think this is what Jesus would be doing if he were in your context. Is this how Jesus would go about incarnating the kingdom in your area? Record your observations in two columns—one for *yes*, one for *no*. How can the activities and habits that fall into the *no* column be reshaped? What activities should you stop altogether? What clutter can you discard? Lastly, ask what else there is that hasn't been thought of. What would Jesus do that you have not even considered.

- Every time you gather, remind one another that you are meeting in the name of Jesus. Some communities we know light a single candle every time they meet to represent the ongoing presence of Jesus among them and to signify that Jesus is the Light of the World. You might even leave an empty chair in the room to remind you of his presence.

Practice Three: Shape Missional Engagement on Jesus

Not only should we pattern our spirituality on Jesus, but we should shape our missional engagement on him as well. In fact, mission is really just an extension or a by-product of a spirituality based on Jesus. His spirituality was one formed around his mission—and it was rugged enough to sustain him in the rough and tumble of his life. If every Christian engaged people as meaningfully, attentively, and redemptively as Jesus did, we would revolutionize the world in no time. Jesus is our primary model of mission. He *is* the Seeker and Savior of the lost.

- Hold Jesus up as the prime example of evangelist, social activist, and missionary. As a community, examine Jesus in the throes of missional engagement. Look at the ways he engaged people, asked questions, listened, and conversed. What can we learn from Jesus? Together, explore, reflect, pray, and seek to emulate him.

- A study into John 5:17–20 will reveal profound insights into how Jesus followed his own Father into mission. This is a great passage to explore together as a group.
- Modeling our missional engagement on Jesus will mean acting like him in relation to those beyond the faith. We have already noted that he was known as the friend of outcasts and sinners and spent lots of time with those not of the faith.
- Here are a few good questions to ask and reflect upon:
  Q. *Whom did Jesus spend time with? Whom do we spend time with?*
  Q. *Whom did Jesus eat with? Whom do we eat with? Whom do we invite to our table?*

Practice Four: Shape Leadership on Jesus

Not only should we pattern our spirituality and missional engagement on Jesus, but we should also shape our leadership and leadership development in light of his example. As we suggest later, in the disciple-making chapter, leadership is an extension of discipleship, the aim of which is to become more like Jesus. There we note that the quality of the church's leadership is directly related to the quality of its discipleship. If we fail in making disciples, we will undoubtedly fail in shaping leaders. Leadership emerges from healthy discipleship and, to be genuinely Christian, must always reflect Christlikeness.

- Jesus had no positional or institutional power; rather, he had moral and spiritual authority. This is the basis of biblical leadership. Spiritual authority emerges from our relationship with God and is given depth through our calling and personal integrity.
- In developing and commissioning leaders, we should focus on character rather than gifting and ability. Spiritual leadership is influence through relationships, not by power or position.
- Build leadership development on top of a healthy disciple-making process. If we get discipleship right, then we are well positioned to develop leaders (see disciple-making section for more information).

- Read the Gospels, and explore Jesus's model of leadership and leadership development. Discuss as a community and seek to integrate those qualities in your own processes.
- Circulate thought-provoking ideas, articles, and books on Christ-centered leadership. *In the Name of Jesus: Reflections on Christian Leadership*, by Henri Nouwen,[8] is a stirring book that highlights Jesus's servant leadership.
- Develop a list of leadership habits and qualities evident in Jesus, to use as a template in shaping all leaders in the group. Periodically use this list as an inventory and a self-evaluation tool for every leader.

Habit 2: Get over Dualism

We have already noted that there was an abiding authenticity to the early believers' faith that permeated every aspect of their individual and collective lives. Following Jesus effectively excluded all other claims to loyalty. If we honestly seek the same level of authentic faith, we will need to dethrone dualism in our lives.

Practice One: All-of-Life Alignment

The first practice we suggest in our efforts to dethrone dualism is the practice of *all-of-life alignment*. When we say *all-of-life alignment*, we recommend a radical realigning of every aspect of our individual and collective lives around Jesus, his ways and purposes. Seeking to embrace an all-of-life perspective and aligning all areas of life under Jesus deposes dualism as it begins to dismantle the false barrier between the sacred and the secular. It creates a seamless experience between faith and life.

- Evaluate your collective activities and structures using the two diagrams above as a template (the diagrams with the three circles). Do your actions and structures fit into the dualistic template or the all-of-life one? What will it mean to realign the elements that fit into the dualistic framework so that all three components—God, world, and church—are integrated?

Missio Dei

A faith community called Missio Dei upholds the practice of outer transformation. They say, "A commitment to outer transformation is a commitment to
ordering our lives around God's transforming dream." A significant part of this
practice for them is to aim at one act of outward transformation each week
that includes vocational alignment. This essentially is a commitment to allow
God's kingdom agenda to order their vocation and working lives.[9]

- Create an all-of-life inventory. Seek to identify the idols in your
  individual and collective lives. Be honest, confess to God and one
  another, and together seek ways to loosen their grip. Develop
  lifestyle habits and practices that guide you in the opposite
  direction. For example, if one of the gods was money and consumerism, then there are very specific things you can commit
  to together as a way to combat this powerful god. Here are a
  few ideas:
    * Every month have a "buy nothing day."
    * Show one another your credit card statements at the end of
      the month (we actually know a community that does this—
      scary, huh?).
    * Issue the challenge to abstain from buying coffee, alcohol, or
      fast food for a week and to give the money away. One of the
      best ways to break the spiritual power of money is to give it
      away.
    * A friend of ours issued a one-week challenge to everyone in
      her church. Knowing that many people in the world survive
      on only one dollar a day for food, the challenge was to keep
      the cost of meals as low as possible. This activity would
      surely challenge our use and abuse of both money and food.
- Establish a practice of vocational (work) alignment. If we believe
  that every aspect of life should be brought under the lordship of
  Jesus, then surely this includes our careers. Are we giving our best
  to wrong causes? Is there space for service in our lives? Can we
  downsize and scale back in order to focus on spiritually significant

things? Seeing that many of us spend close to a third of our days at work, this should be a priority.

Practice Two: Hallow the Everyday

Secondly, in deposing dualism in our lives, we suggest the practice of attempting to hallow (make holy) the everyday activities of life. This idea comes directly from the Hebraic understanding that there are only two realities in the world: the *holy* and the *not-yet-holy*, and that the task of God's people is to make the not-yet-holy into that which is holy. Here are some suggestions.

- Together, explore this Hebraic view of life. A good place to start is chapter 7 of *The Shaping of Things to Come* (especially p. 132).
- Hallowing the everyday is achieved by seeking to focus and direct our daily tasks toward God and his purposes, not away from him. It's about intentionality, mindfulness, and purpose.

The Redemption
of Pleasure

Because of its innate dualism, Western Christianity has generally struggled to integrate pleasure, passion, and instinctive drives into the faith. There exists no framework to connect pleasure with God. You don't have to search long to discover this distortion in relation to sex, food, and other forms of pleasure. It is our belief that the skewed ascetic perspective fueled by dualism has deeply alienated the average person from Christianity by failing to help them integrate their bodies and associated physical life into a spiritual experience of God. We cannot underestimate the damage that this life suppression has done to the way we are perceived by the average non-Christian, not to mention the fact that it represents a distortion of the biblical view of the world. It also highlights the need to recover a redemptive framework for pleasure as a missional asset. We would do well to remember that people are motivated by their deepest pleasures, and if we can connect these to God, we will have established a vital bridge into the lives of those around us. Pleasure can be a greater motivator for God.[10]

- A good question to explore as a group is, "How can we make sacred our everyday ordinary tasks?" How can cleaning be made holy? Shopping? Work? Meeting for lunch? Study? And so on. You'll be surprised at the interesting and meaningful suggestions people will discover simply by dreaming and brainstorming together. Here are a couple of examples: "How can we hallow our eating?" Eat with thankfulness, respect, generosity, and moderation. Eat with those beyond the faith, your neighbors, friends, the lonely, the poor, and so on. "How can we hallow our recreation?" Use the time and context to connect with people, to serve others, to be refreshed, to reflect on God, to connect with creation.

- Start to define holiness positively by what we actively *do* in hallowing the everyday, not by what we *don't* do. This viewpoint leads to a more life-affirming approach to holiness. This is exactly the holiness of Jesus—it seeks to change the world and sanctify it.

- Seek to integrate within the community the value that *all of life is sacred* and can/should be directed toward God. Talk about it regularly, and begin to live it out together. Seek to engage and redeem culture rather than avoiding it.

- Develop a theology that redeems pleasure and traces it back to God, its originator. This will become an important missional asset, as explained in *The Redemption of Pleasure* excerpt.

Practice Three: Redefine and Widen Your View of Worship

Directly connected to hallowing the everyday is the practice of redefining and widening our view of worship. Keeping in mind that there is no divide between the sacred and secular, a biblical expression of worship can and should occur in all spheres of life. It should not be reduced to a certain time and place, namely, a few hours a week inside a church building. While there is inherently nothing wrong with gathering as a group of believers to express our adoration and love, if this is all that constitutes our worship, we're probably in the thrall of dualism. In fact, this is one of the more influential practices that perpetuate dualism in our midst. Remember the diagrams above. All of life belongs to God, and true worship means bringing every sphere under him. So even though we might gather weekly for corporate worship, we must widen our view and practices.

- A good place to start is to ask the question, "What is worship?" Study the scriptures, explore what Jesus taught, read other perspectives, and together redefine and broaden your understanding and practice of worship.

- Encourage people in your group to share with one another the ways in which they are seeking to worship God outside of the regular corporate gatherings. This could become a great resource for your congregation.

- Alan's definition of worship is "offering our world back to God." This is an all-encompassing definition that incorporates *all of life* into worship—our time, money, resources, pleasures, voices, work, and the like, including our times of gathering together.

- To stir the imagination a little, we recommend reading and discussing chapters 12 and 13 in Michael Frost's book *Exiles*. Here, Michael outlines authentic worship as listed in a set of ways in which we *love* God.[11] He suggests we love and worship God by

Releasing the Glory of God

One of the most wonderful metaphors in Jewish spirituality is the rabbinical teaching on the Shekinah (God's glory). Some Jewish mysticism presents the Shekinah in a playful way, with the form of a woman and a personality. She is metaphorically portrayed as God's wife in exile, that is, God and his glory have been tragically separated through the fall. The separation is one of a cosmic crash in which God's glory was scattered into myriad sparks and caught up in all created matter. The holy sparks are now imprisoned in all things. The remarkable aspect of this Jewish teaching is the view that it is our holy actions—that is, actions filled with holy intent and directed toward God—that actually free the holy sparks ensnared in all things and allow the exiled Shekinah to journey back to her Husband. God and his glory are joined together again when people act in holiness. Now, without taking the teaching as literal truth (most rabbis don't), this is a helpful way of viewing the mission of God's people in the world. When we act redemptively and in holiness, we fan into flames the creational purpose that lies at the heart of all things in God's world—we liberate God's glory that lies in it. And in so doing we bring God glory.[12]

* loving others
* obeying Jesus
* lingering in God's company
* speaking about the things of God
* longing for the return of Christ
* forsaking other gods and idols
* laying down our life
* loving what God has created
* forgiving others

Now that's what we mean by a wide and all-embracing, seamless approach to worship that seeks to orient *all of life* under the lordship of Christ.

Habit 3: Make the Gospels the Primary Text

The third habit we suggest in keeping Jesus at the core of our collective consciousness and action is to make the Gospels our primary texts. In the same way that the remarkable movements clung to the gospel and linked their faith in utter simplicity to Christ, Jesus ought to be the prism through which we view our world. The Gospels, therefore, give us a primary orientation and function as principal texts for mission and discipleship. This is not to say we neglect the other sections of scripture, but rather that we read the *entire* counsel of God in reference to the Gospels. These are the narratives that shape and define us, essentially because they are the primary record of Jesus's life and teaching.

Practice One: Recalibrate around Jesus's Core Teaching

In keeping Jesus at the heart and in making the Gospels our primary text, we should specifically home in on Jesus's central teaching and seek to recalibrate all our learning and activity around these truths. This means we should not only spend a lot of time in the Gospels' narratives, but particularly meditate upon the words and teachings of our Lord.

• As a community explore the parables Jesus told, and seek to integrate these truths into everyday life.

- Explore what Jesus said about certain themes such as prayer or money or heaven or hell.
- Study the Sermon on the Mount in depth. What do these truths mean for us today?

Alan, in his book *ReJesus* (coauthored with Michael Frost),[13] outlines a simple way in which to process the content and implications of Jesus's core teaching. The book provides a table with three columns exploring the core aspects of Jesus's teaching and life, the implications for discipleship and church, and ideas and examples of how this can be lived out. What follows is an excerpt from that table. This is not exhaustive but is an example of how a group can explore the central ideas and implications of Jesus's teaching. It's a great exercise in seeking to recalibrate around Jesus and his central teachings. You can use this same process in your own explorations.

Aspect of Jesus's Life and Teaching	Implication for Disciple/Church	Possible Example of How These Could Be Lived Out
Ushered in the kingdom of God and focused it around his own person (e.g., Mark 1:14–15; Luke 11:20).	The kingdom of God is central and extends in and beyond the church to his entire cosmos. We are agents of the kingdom in all spheres of life common to human being. Jesus is Lord/King! We can live and work wherever we are, and we can expect the kingdom to already be there.	When we are at work, we invite Jesus to accompany us there. We look for opportunities to enact Jesus's qualities while we are working. We look for ways to mirror the work of God even through the most mundane and everyday activities.
Mediates the grace and mercy of God (e.g., Matt. 12:7).	Openness to receive as well as impart grace/mercy to others. The measure we give will be the measure we receive. We can be generous with both our resources and our time. God is merciful; we must try to find ways to be like God in daily life.	We refuse to rule out the unlikely agents of grace in our midst. Whether someone is uneducated, elderly, divorced, an ex-convict, disabled, or even just needy or annoying, we humbly accept their gifts to us as if they were from God.
Offers forgiveness of sins (e.g., Matt. 9:2; Luke 7:47).	Repentance and forgiveness are a way of life (70x7). Radical openness to a holy God will require that we be constantly aware of our sinfulness and the possibility of radical evil that lurks in the human soul. Also, we must be a forgiving people (Matt. 6:15).	We examine ourselves carefully for any bitterness or lack of forgiveness toward others. We place ourselves in relationships of accountability. We are open to the rebuke of the loving friend. We confess our limitations regularly.

Continued

Aspect of Jesus's Life and Teaching	Implication for Disciple/Church	Possible Example of How These Could Be Lived Out
Demonstrates the love of God for his world (e.g., John 3:16; 14:21).	Demands our primary love for God and a secondary love for others in his name. We need to know we are a loved people, and this should be expressed towards others. This love should include but extend beyond our family members to embrace even our enemies. We should be known as a people of love.	We show love to our family members and do so reflecting on the way it is an outpouring of the love we have received from God. We practice hospitality to the stranger. We create spaces in which others can grow and find grace.
Radicalizes the current standards of holiness (e.g., the Sermon on the Mount, Matt. 5–8).	Jesus sets a challenging ethical and moral code for the disciple/church to follow. The Sermon on the Mount is the most-used discipleship text in the history of the church. This not only describes but prescribes the life of discipleship. We should make it a basic reference text and seek to live it out.	We practice hospitality, generosity, humility, and justice. We believe our faith brings not just personal salvation but a motivation for changing the world to reflect the justice and peace of God.
Proclaims (as well as lives) the good news of the kingdom (e.g., Matt. 5:13–16).	We should proclaim (as well as live) the good news of Jesus. In a sense we are (and must become) good news (we are salt/light). Love, forgiveness, mercy, compassion, righteous anger . . . these are the marks of a disciple.	We socialize with unbelievers. We pray for them. We model an alternate reality by our alternate lifestyle. We are always ready to give an answer for the hope within us. We acknowledge the ministry of the gifted evangelists among us.

Practice Two: Cycle through the Gospels

An effective way to make the Gospels the primary text for your community is to establish a practice where as many people as possible are reading the Gospels over and over again. This is what we mean by cycling through the Gospels (we're not telling you to get on your bike!).

- Set up a routine where everyone can read the same Gospel in the same time period. This will help people to ask one another how they are doing in their reading and to discuss the content. Maybe you can assign a Gospel per month. This way each participant will read all four Gospels three times in the year. Encourage discussion, feedback, journaling, and prayer.
- Every time you meet as a small group, read through a section from the Gospels.

- A church in Melbourne, Australia, hosts regular walks through the city, stopping at the casino, parliament house, the business and banking center, skid row, and so on. At these places they read among themselves certain sections of the Gospel of Mark. This not only helps people become familiar with the gospel but sheds new light as they read and reflect right in the hustle and bustle of the city.

- Organize a Stations of the Cross reflection at Easter. This tradition, which began with St. Francis of Assisi, helps people to meditate upon the chief scenes of Christ's sufferings and death, through an in-depth contemplation on the final hours (or Passion) of Jesus as recorded in the Gospels. This is a great way to help people enter into the biblical narrative in a profound manner.[14]

Practice Three: Keep the Gospels Central to Your Learning

As we have seen, Deuteronomy 6:4 requires that our core beliefs and commitments are to become part of the fabric of our everyday lives. We are to impress them on our children, talk about them when we sit at home and walk along the road, when we lie down and when we get up. We are to have them as symbols on our hands (representing everything we do) and bind them on our foreheads (signifying everything we think). Not only that, but we are to write them on the door frames of our homes and on our gates. The bottom line is that the essence of our faith is to be integrated in the hub of life—through the daily activities and conversations between the members of the faith community. If the Gospels of Jesus are the core narratives that shape and define us, they must become central to our learning as a community, both formally and informally.

- Keep Jesus and the Gospels the focus of all your reading, teaching, and exploration of scripture. Both Old and New Testaments point to Jesus as the focal point of God's revelation and redemption. Reducing the Bible to moral instruction, without Jesus and the Gospels as the central message, is to bypass the core purpose of scripture. There are great resources available, such as Graeme Goldsworthy's *According to God's Plan*,[15] to help retain this focus.

- Each year explore one of the Gospels in reasonable depth. To maximize the learning, you could coordinate your large-group and small-group gatherings to be studying the same Gospel at the same time. This will enable both large- and small-group processing as well as give more time for reflection.

- Invite a specialist on the Gospels (such as a New Testament professor or seminary lecturer) to run a series of informative and practical workshops for your group. From there you could take

Third Place Communities

As mentioned in the preface, Third Place Communities (TPC) is the network of missional communities that Darryn cofounded. TPC will function as a test case throughout this book. Please keep in mind that we are not holding TPC up as a superior example; we are simply more familiar with them than with other communities. They have also been working at integrating the forgotten ways theory into their practice, thus providing us with plenty of examples. In seeking to keep Jesus as the central focus in their mission, TPC have experimented with a number of practices and approaches. Here are a few examples:

- TPC encourage all members to cycle through the Gospels each year.
- Together they have sought fresh perspectives on Jesus and have explored a Hebraic view of faith. All new participants are encouraged to read related articles and books.
- All in the community are encouraged to read a few standard texts on Christ and mission.
- TPC have compiled an extensive resource of DVD presentations on the Gospels and other elements of Christology. These are passed around, viewed together, and discussed.
- Periodically, a specialist has been invited to partake in workshops and seminars.
- They have designed and printed hundreds of *What Would Jesus Brew* t-shirts. While this is a little tongue-in-cheek humor, it also functions as a reminder that Jesus is always active in brewing something in the world (if you want to see the design or grab your own shirt check out http://www.cafepress.com/wwjbapparel). They have also summarized their core practices into this question: "What is Jesus brewing within, amongst and around?" (more on this later).

the information presented and process it over time through your small-group structure.

- Host seminars on how to get the most out of reading the Gospels. This could be as simple as providing basic principles in studying them, or by offering examples of reading all scripture in light of Jesus and the Gospels.
- Set up a system where every week a portion of the Gospels is e-mailed or text-messaged to each person in the group. If everyone is receiving and reading the same excerpt from the Gospels, it's sure to flow into some of the everyday conversations.

Group Processing

Session 1: *Explore (talk about it)*

- If you had to highlight one idea from this section, what would it be? Why?

- In your own words, explain the concept of "Jesus is Lord" to another person in the group. What ideas excite you? Concern you?

- What are the best habits and practices to consider? We have provided a few. Can you think of any others?

- What questions do you have?

- How can you imagine the group growing in this area?

Session 2: *Evaluate (reflect deeper)*

- Is the practice of Jesus as Lord a strength or a weakness for your group?

- Does the majority of the group understand and believe in this concept?

- How is commitment to these ideas already demonstrated in your group? Give examples.

- When was the community best at keeping Jesus as Lord? What were the contributing factors?

- In your opinion, what are the most important issues in keeping Jesus as Lord?

- What challenges are ahead? What are the barriers? Where do you anticipate resistance?

Session 3: *Employ (act on it)*

- What needs to happen during the next twelve months? What do you need to do that you're not currently doing?

- What will you need to let go of?

- What information and resources will you need? Who else needs to be involved?

- How will you know if you have grown in these areas? What will the key indicators be?

- What habits and practices will you seek to integrate during the next twelve months? List them here.

Action Plans

What are the first steps you will take to achieve these goals? Looking at your past, are they realistic?

What—Activity/Action	When—Date	Who—Leader/Participants
1.		
2.		
3.		
4.		

Session 4: *Personal Journal*

After processing much information, take some time to pray, listen, and respond to God. How is God prompting you and how will you respond? Take time to record your impressions as well as insights from the group. Write a prayer expressing your desires to God. If appropriate, share your thoughts in the group, and then pray together.

- What am I sensing from God?

- What is my prayer?

3

Disciple Making

The Importance of Disciple Making

As we have already indicated, all the elements of mDNA belong together and must be present in significant ways for authentic Apostolic Genius to activate. But disciple making is perhaps the most critical element in the mDNA mix, because it involves the critical task of becoming more like our Founder, Jesus—of actually embodying what he was about. When dealing with discipleship, and the related capacity to generate authentic followers of Jesus, we are dealing with the crucial factor that will in the end determine the quality of the whole—if we fail at this point, then we are almost guaranteed to fail in all the others. It is such a critical task that Jesus focused most of his energy on it. The most significant religious movement in history was initiated through the simple act of Jesus investing his life in a small motley group of believers, growing them into authentic disciples. For the follower of Jesus, discipleship is not the first step in a promising career, but the fulfillment of their destiny to be conformed to the image of Christ (Rom. 8:29).

When we look at the stories of Christian movements that change the world, we can say that they are simply disciple-making systems. Everyone is involved at all levels of the community. Disciple making is the starting point, the primary practice, and a very significant key to lasting missional impact. Whether one looks at the Celtic, Wesleyan, Franciscan, or Chinese phenomena, at their core they are led by disciples who are absolutely committed in turn to reproducing disciples.

In contrast, the church in the West has largely forgotten the art of disciple making and has largely reduced it to an intellectual assimilation of theological ideas. As a result, we have a rather anemic cultural Christianity highly susceptible to the lures of consumerism. This in turn works directly against a true following of Jesus. In our desire to be seeker-friendly and attractional, we have largely abandoned the vigorous kind of discipleship that characterized early Christianity and every significant Jesus movement since.

Neil Cole of Church Multiplication Associates (CMA) suggests that the key to CMA's remarkable growth revolved around precisely this issue—reproducing disciples. They adopt the approach of *lowering the bar of how church is done and raising the bar of what it means to be a disciple.*[1] Their reasoning is that if the way we conceive and structure church is simple enough that anyone can reproduce it, and is made up of people who follow Jesus at any cost, the result will be a movement that empowers the common Christian to do the uncommon works of God. In contrast, it seems that many of our current practices seem to run contrary to this—we make church complex and discipleship too easy.

The Challenge of Consumerism

Discipleship is about adherence to Christ and therefore is articulated and embraced over against all other competing claims for our loyalty. It is suggested that the major challenge to our allegiance today, and thus a serious threat to discipleship, is that of consumerism. There is little doubt that in consumerism we are dealing with a very significant religious phenomenon. If the role of religion is to offer a sense of identity, purpose, meaning, and community, then it can be said that consumerism is a type of religion. Much that goes by the name of advertising is an explicit offer of identity, meaning, purpose, community, and significance. Most marketing strategies appeal to one or more of these religious impulses.

The challenge for the church in this situation is that it is forced to compete with the other invitations for our allegiance and in the end can become just another vendor of goods and services. The church operating in an attractional mode, primarily run by professionals, has always been susceptible to this lure. Furthermore, under the influence of church growth practice, consumerism became the driving ideology of the church's ministry. Its proponents taught us how to market and tailor the church to suit target audiences. By failing to intentionally focus on making disciples, we inadvertently cultivated religious consumerism.

The Embodiment of Jesus

What did Jesus have in mind when he commissioned the church to make disciples of all nations?[2] A missional understanding of this commission requires us to see Jesus's tactic as to mobilize a whole lot of little versions of himself infiltrating every nook and cranny of society. He seeks to do this by reproducing himself in and through his people. Jesus not only embodies God amongst us, but also provides the image of the perfect human being. Paul tells us that it is our eternal destiny to be conformed to the image of Christ.[3] All the spiritual disciplines therefore aim us toward one thing—*Christlikeness*. It is the essential task of discipleship to embody the mission and character of Jesus.

The dangerous stories of Jesus are alive in his people, and in a very real way, we must actually *become the gospel* to the people around us. When we look at the phenomenal movements, we find that these groups found a way to translate the grand themes of the gospel into concrete life through the embodiment of Jesus in ways that were profoundly relational and attractive. This embodiment cannot be passed on through books: it is always communicated through life itself, by the leader to the community, from teacher to disciple, and from believer to believer.

The Power of Spiritual Leadership and Discipleship

Gandhi, the inspirational leader who transformed India, never held political office or headed up a government. And yet he transformed his people and altered the world, not by the normal exercise of power, but through sheer inspirational power based on religious, moral, and social virtues. He based his message solely on what he called moral authority, what we may call spiritual authority or inspirational leadership.

Inspirational leadership can be described as a unique type of social power that comes from the personal integration and embodiment of great ideas, as opposed to power that comes from external authority like that of government, corporations, or religious institutions. It involves a relationship between leaders and followers in which each influences the other to pursue common objectives, with the aim of transforming followers into leaders in their own right. Spiritual authority arises from one's relationship to God and is shaped by one's calling, gifting, and personal integrity. It is a noncoercive power that influences people through spiritual power—it draws people into its influence and changes them by calling out a moral and spiritual response in those who respond.

Here's the rub: the quality of the church's leadership is directly proportional to the quality of its discipleship. If we fail in the area of making disciples, we should not be surprised if we fail in leadership development. Discipleship is primary; leadership is always secondary. And leadership, to be genuinely Christian, must always reflect Christlikeness and, therefore, discipleship.

Hitting the Road with Jesus

Unfortunately, the church has often replaced life-on-life discipleship with institutional learning based on the principle that if people get the right information, they will change their behavior. This is trying to *think our way into a new way of acting.* Jesus's approach to discipleship is based on the idea that we need to change people's behavior, and their thinking will follow. In other words, we need to *act our way into a new way of thinking.* What we are proposing looks something like this:

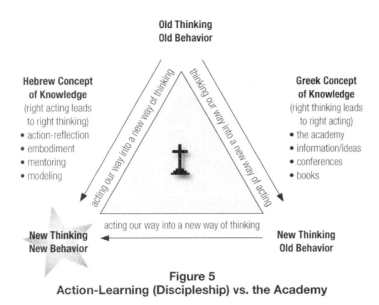

Figure 5
Action-Learning (Discipleship) vs. the Academy

The disciples hit the road with Jesus and learned about discipleship in the rough-and-tumble of life and mission. Let's look at a few suggested disciple-making practices that do the same.

Suggested Habits and Practices

In tackling the various habits and practices associated with disciple making, please note that what follows is not an exhaustive list of individual spiritual disciplines central to discipleship. There are people far more qualified for this task (see the writings of Richard Foster and Dallas Willard, for instance). The focus here, however, will be on creating a *disciple-making environment* for missional communities. Our aim is to construct a broad framework of habits and practices core to setting up a system for discipleship and disciple making. In this light we suggest the following habits and connected practices.

1. Raise the bar on discipleship
2. Develop a set of discipleship practices
3. Activate the priesthood of all believers

Habit 1: Raise the Bar on Discipleship

The first habit we suggest in creating a healthy disciple-making system is to establish specific, well-articulated discipleship standards or norms for your community. These norms will convey what is expected of each member of the community. As such, they should address what is *normative* for Christian discipleship. In doing this, seek to address the question, "What is the everyday requirement for those who consider themselves Christian?" In addition to these basic discipleship commitments, groups may like to add their own norms unique to their context (as seen in the examples in the resource section).

We also suggest that in establishing the standard of discipleship you ensure that mission is a non-negotiable part of what it means to be a disciple. Prevailing conceptions of discipleship rarely focus on mission. Unfortunately, it's often viewed as an optional element within the disciple-making process. However, if we are true to our vocation to fashion a community to continue Jesus's missionary endeavor, mission must become the central theme and organizing principle for discipleship. This is exactly how Jesus formed his disciples, thoroughly around the call to mission. As soon as the disciples were called, Jesus took them on a journey of mission and learning. Straightaway they were involved in proclaiming the kingdom, serving the poor, healing, and casting out demons. It was active and direct disciple making in the context of mission. Even the newest believer should be engaged in mission from the start.

Practice One: Make Discipleship Real Discipleship

In *An Unstoppable Force*, Erwin McManus says that what we have viewed in the past as extraordinary Christianity should in fact be the *radical minimum standard* for all Christians. He writes: "The measure of an apostolic community is not in the legends created by heroic acts but in the quality and texture of what that community considers ordinary living."[4] He considers it a mistake when we make heroes out of those who were simply living a normal Christian life. We confuse the bare minimum with the extraordinary and keep lowering the bar until we clear it. McManus proposes that there may be no more significant ingredient to an apostolic ethos than establishing a *radical minimum standard* for discipleship.[5]

This will definitely mean raising the bar of current discipleship norms. Jesus called us to deny ourselves, pick up our cross, and follow him. He called us to love God with all our heart, soul, and mind, and to love our neighbors as ourselves. According to God's word, this is basic Christianity. It should be normal for Christians to be hospitable and spend regular time with those beyond the faith. It ought to be typical to be generous with our time and money, to love extravagantly, to care for creation, and share our faith. If you scratch beneath the surface of the many influential Christian movements, you will find a common commitment to this type of radical Christian living.

Astute mission groups will establish a high minimum discipleship standard and ensure it becomes part of the ethos and fabric of the community.

- To do this, make certain that these basic discipleship commitments are ingrained in the church's culture and way of life.
- Later, we will point out that culture is formed primarily through the daily conversations and interactions among the church members. So, in order to embed a discipleship standard, it needs to be talked about regularly as well as enacted.
- Together, as a community, explore the scriptures, pray, collaborate, and establish a radical minimum discipleship norm.

Practice Two: Promote Core Spiritual Disciplines

While we've stated previously that the goal in this section is not to provide a comprehensive list of spiritual practices, we feel we must include a basic list of what we understand to be the core *non-negotiable* disciplines for all Christians, if they are to grow into authentic disciples.

- *Engagement with scripture*
  We begin with engaging the Word of God as a core discipline. In many ways this is a no-brainer, but a discipline that all too often gets left on the shelf—literally! And it is possible to study the Bible and miss the central theme of discipleship and disciple making. The emphasis, therefore, should not simply be on right thinking but on right action. Rather than asking, "*What can I get out of*

this?" we must ask a new question: "How do the scriptures call, shape, transform, and send us?"[6] As Darrell Guder suggests, "The Bible must continue to confront, to convert, and to transform the community for faithful witness."[7]

As we advise further in this book, by exploring salvation history described through scripture, the faith community will be able to find itself as part of this ongoing redemptive story. It's imperative to engage scripture this way as a living text. This is why Paul writes to Timothy, his son in the faith, that all scripture is God-breathed and useful for teaching and training in righteousness, so that the disciple may be thoroughly equipped for every good work.[8]

* Read scripture every time you gather, from planning meetings, to small groups, to large gatherings.
* Provide resources such as study materials, DVDs, reading plans, and the like.
* Seek commitment from the community to read a certain number of chapters per week.
* Every day, e-mail or text-message a passage from scripture to each community member.
* Periodically, host intensives on specific books of the Bible or on biblical themes. Invite an experienced teacher from outside the community to become part of the learning experience.

We have found the Catholic tradition of *praying the scriptures*[9] helpful, along with journaling and meditation. We've also used Edward de Bono's Six Thinking Hats framework as a different way to explore the Bible.[10] There are many ways in which to engage the scriptures, so be creative, and together explore new approaches and customs.

• *Prayer*
Second, we promote personal and communal prayer as non-negotiable for discipleship. Within the practice of prayer we would include solitude, stillness, contemplation, and petition, as well as confession. Philip Yancey suggests that prayer is the most fundamental, challenging, perplexing, and deeply rewarding aspect of our relationship with God.[11]

* Pray every time you meet with others.
* Create a "prayer of the week" that the entire community commits to each day.
* Pray at every meal.
* Educate people about prayer through teaching and books and other helpful resources.

It's important to foster prayer at all levels, individually and corporately, and become a community in regular conversation with God. Spice it up a little and explore different approaches and traditions of prayer, such as the ancient Catholic tradition of examen.[12]

- *Worship and service*

The next core practice essential for disciple making is the twin discipline of worship and service. In fact, because we view worship as ultimately *offering our world back to God*, it incorporates the vow to service—we see them as one and the same. The practice of worship and service includes commitments to participating in ministry, utilizing spiritual gifts, acts of kindness, generosity, evangelism, pursuing justice, and tithing, as well as meeting with the faith community for communion, praise, celebration, learning, and expression. Again, there are a myriad of ways these commitments can be expressed; the important thing is that they are indeed practiced.

- *Stewardship*

Stewardship is essentially about each Christian taking personal responsibility for the way he or she uses money, resources, and time, as well as caring for God's creation. In today's climate of consumerism and environmental issues, followers of Christ must exemplify a simple and prophetic life-response to the issues of our day. Here are a few ideas to consider.

* Watch your use of time and money. Keep one another accountable.
* Job share or work part-time if possible. Release your time for family, friends, and ministry.

* Share your resources with those around you. Rent or buy a house with others.
* Consider the impact your investments have on the environment. What companies benefit from our investment? What do they produce? Are they ethical and environmentally aware?
* Explore the theme of advocacy. How do we represent and lead against what is wrong in our world? How can we become God's representatives against injustice?
* Get involved in environmental concerns. Recycle, avoid unnecessary waste, watch your use of nonrenewable energy, and carpool, walk, or ride a bike if possible.
* Consider the foods and other products you buy. Are they from ethical companies? What impact do production and distribution have on the poor and their local environment?
* Educate your community about the current environmental issues. Provide resources and examples. Regularly share what people are doing to live simply and care for the earth.

You get the idea. Work out what is best for you and your community, and become responsible, caring stewards of your things and creation.

• *Community*
The final practice central to discipleship is a deep-seated commitment to community. Following Jesus and growing in his likeness cannot be accomplished alone. A call to Christ is a clear summoning to participate in his community. In fact, we see it not only as a commitment but as a spiritual discipline.

The two most common metaphors used in scripture to describe the church are that of the family (household) and the "body of Christ." We are all part of the body of Christ and should have equal concern for one another. If one part suffers, every part suffers; if one part is honored, every part rejoices with it.[13] Paul writes that as one body we are held together by every supporting ligament as each part does its work to grow and be built up in love.[14] Jesus set a high standard of devotion to community. He gave us a new commandment to love one another in the same way he loved us, and by doing so people will know that we are his true disciples.[15] As you can see, commitment to community has far-reaching impact and at the end of the day is highly missional.

Habit 2: Develop a Set of Discipleship Practices

Discipleship practices are basically a set of practical commitments that guide a community in living and growing together as disciples. These practices are best developed through a community-wide collaborative process where all members get the opportunity to have input. This way the practices will receive broader ownership and commitment.

In essence the practices should be shaped by and flow from the specific minimum discipleship standards previously established. We also recommend incorporating these practices with the missional practices mentioned in chapter five. This, then, becomes an intentional way for a community to live out their call and commitment to discipleship *and* disciple making.

Practice One: Create Common Practices

In setting up a healthy disciple-making environment, we recommend developing a set of community discipleship practices. All groups would benefit greatly from this as a way to engage in discipleship in a collective and sustainable manner. Developing practices will also shift discipleship from a programmed activity to a lifestyle and will give everyone in the community a clear framework of how they can participate. Practices create a distinct culture and set a rhythm that shapes communal life.

The leadership task is to

- Educate the group on the importance of discipleship practices.
- Explain that as disciples we act our way into a new way of thinking rather than the other way around.
- Guide the collaborative process in developing the common practices.

- Ensure the practices are connected with the overall unique calling for your church.

The process

1. Identify core values through group discussion, prayer, and reflection. These are the values that really grab the community. This process requires that you identify the values and beliefs that are non-negotiable and inspire passion. It might take some time, and we encourage you not to rush it. Many will already have done this, and therefore can jump to #2.
2. Establish your minimum discipleship standards.
3. Brainstorm the different ways these norms and values can be practiced in everyday life. It is important that the group identify everyday things, not just "religious" activities, with the practices. For example, the core value of hospitality might be expressed in eating regularly with Christians and non-Christians or in regularly having the poor in your home. Eating is thus transformed into a culture-making, missional activity. List many possible ways a core value can be embodied.
4. Choose only one or two key practices for each. Make sure they're achievable and realistic while still raising the bar on discipleship. The practices should require some discipline and commitment.
5. Develop a memorable acronym or simple way to phrase the practices. This is very important, because if they are not easy to remember, people won't practice them.
6. Expect a common commitment to the practices from all stakeholders. Be careful of legalism, but also don't lower the bar to simply suit middle-class sensibilities. These practices should entice *and* challenge us.

For examples of discipleship practices, see the resource section at the end of the book.

Practice Two: Develop a Contagious Discipleship Culture

This is essentially about working toward a critical mass of individuals within the community who take their discipleship and disciple making seriously enough to make its practice a priority in their lives. The idea is that if you get enough people within a group behaving a certain way, it's bound to influence and tip the remaining members in the same direction.

If you can mobilize enough people to engage in healthy disciple-making practices, it will have a flow-on effect within the rest of your community. For example, if you can encourage one-quarter of your members to meet regularly in small groups for prayer and accountability, the scales are sure to tip in that direction. When discipleship is expected of everyone, and enough key people are involved in the practices, it will create a culture where discipleship is accepted as the norm and the desired goal.

- *Talk about and Expect Growth* Word-of-mouth is one of the most powerful activities in which to engender change. Our environment is significantly shaped by what we talk about. So it makes sense that to fashion an ethos and culture for spiritual growth, we need to talk about it regularly. Teach it from the scriptures, speak about it in everyday conversation, provide tangible examples, encourage people to share what they are doing and how they are growing as a result.

  By way of regular conversation about the importance of spiritual growth, the community will be reminded of their destiny to become more like Jesus.

DNA Groups at SmallBoatBigSea

In creating an environment for disciple making, SmallBoatBigSea[16] established what they term DNA groups. *DNA* stands for *discipleship, nurture,* and *accountability*. Every person in their midst is encouraged to join a DNA, which is made up of two to five people who meet regularly to talk, support, and pray. DNAs meet in many places: some in cafés or pubs, others in homes, and others on the beach. The groups are encouraged to use their community commitments to guide questions for accountability:[17] This week, whom have you blessed? With whom have you eaten? Have you sensed any promptings from God? What passages of scripture have encouraged you, or what other resources have enriched your growth? In what ways have you sensed yourself carrying on the work of God in your daily life?[18]

If people are not growing in the faith, they should be encouraged by the group to do so.

- *Practice Together*

  Environments are shaped not only by what we talk about, but also by what we do together. Through enacting spiritual practices with others in the church, you will implant a healthy discipleship ethos deep within the community. This will also help us get beyond the individualistic notion of discipleship that pervades Western understandings of church. A simple way for something to become a habit is to do it frequently. And so by acting together as a learning community, people will realize that they're part of a community where it's normal to strive and grow toward Christlikeness.

- *Provide Resources and Tools*

  To help people regularly engage in spiritual disciplines, it's a good idea to provide a bank of resources and tools. We have noticed that people in our communities have benefited greatly from engaging the scriptures and prayer through the Catholic traditions of lectio and examen.[19] These are two excellent and simple spiritual exercises you can hand out or e-mail around your community. In fact, they're so simple you could even text them to others in your community.

  One of the best new tools around is Exilio—a resource based on the book *Exiles* by Michael Frost. It involves thorough group

Life Transformation Groups
at CMA

With the core task of discipleship in mind, Neil Cole, from Church Multiplication Associates,[20] developed Life Transformation Groups, a simple and reproducible disciple-making system involving Bible reading, personal accountability, and prayer. An LTG is made up of two to three people of the same gender, who meet weekly for accountability for their spiritual growth. It is recommended that a group not grow past three, but rather multiply into two groups. In the CMA movement, all are expected to be in an LTG.

reflection and action and includes video material as well.[21] Shape-vine also has a wealth of online resources through the training modules available there.[22] We're sure that without too much effort you could compile an excellent resource library for your group. Study materials, DVDs, information on conferences, Web sites, networks, books, and traditions from other cultures are helpful and within easy reach.

• *Lead by Example*

If you want to set up a culture for spiritual growth, make sure the key leaders and stakeholders model it in their own lives. You simply cannot expect others to engage a way of life that the leaders themselves do not practice. As the saying goes, habits are more easily caught that taught. It's a good idea to set a basic discipleship standard for leaders and stakeholders that is above the minimum standard, as mentioned before. Lead by example and allow others to be inspired to follow.

* Develop a leadership covenant based on agreed-upon norms of discipleship. All leaders should commit to adhering to this covenant.
* Hold one another accountable to the standards set in the covenant.

Habit 3: Activate the Priesthood of All Believers

Movements that change the world are essentially what sociologists call "people movements," that is, they engage all the people as significant agents in the system. Translated to apostolic movements, we can say that every believer is a minister of Jesus Christ and ought to be released as such. This is based squarely on the profound revolutionary doctrine of the priesthood of all believers. Every participant in the Jesus movement is a player, someone who can change the world. God created us this way for this very purpose. Paul highlights this in Ephesians 2:10 when he wrote, "we are God's workmanship, created in Christ Jesus to do good works, which God prepared in advance for us to do." If this is the case, then empowerment is one of the most significant leadership functions.

This is exactly how Jesus personally equipped the first disciples. Not long after initially calling the Twelve, Jesus sent them out into active service, not for menial tasks, but to drive out demons, to heal the sick, and to preach the gospel.[23] Talk about a baptism by fire! And after just three short years, he entrusted to them the entire future of his movement. Now, that's true empowerment! Groups seeking to grow genuine disciples will provide a setting that inspires people to take responsibility for their own growth and exercise of their God-given gifts.

Practice One: Empower People to Utilize Their Gifts

As highlighted in Ephesians 4, disciple making is focused on equipping God's people for works of service so that the body of Christ might mature.[24] It's also clear from scripture that God has individually gifted each believer for this purpose. In fact, God has personally arranged each part of his church and gifted every disciple just the way he wants them to be.[25] Furthermore, we believe that when people discover their gifts and calling, they connect directly with God's purpose for their life. If empowerment is a key leadership function, then helping people locate their gifts, abilities, and passions, and providing a context in which to serve, is the way to do it.

As we suggest in chapter 5, encourage as many people in your community to complete a gift analysis like the one Alan developed at www.theforgottenways.org/apest/.[26] This analysis will profile the primary gifts and calling for each person. It's a helpful place to start, but empowering people to discover and use their gifts is not as simple as answering a few questions and printing off the results. It is not the privilege solely of leadership, but of the whole faith community, to confirm, encourage, and equip people for service. That is why in the online profile tool just mentioned, there is a 360-degree evaluation that invites others around you into the process.

- Encourage those in your community to complete a gift analysis course.
- Map the gifts on a graph or table for a broad overview. Then organize a weekend retreat to explore the map and to brainstorm how these gifts might be used in connection with the group's specific calling.

- Periodically gather those with similar gifts to continue dreaming and encouraging one another to grow and exercise their gifts and calling.
- Locate people's innate passions and energy, and begin to structure mission and ministry around those.
- Commission every member for service in some form or another. Whether in the world of business, health, education, trades, or church, everyone should know they are an agent of the kingdom and should be recognized as such by their faith community. Don't wait too long; as soon as people come to faith, they should become part of the conspiracy of Little Jesuses.

Third Place Communities Coaching

TPC have established a coaching ethos as part of their disciple making. They provide their members with a pool of experienced coaches, many of whom exist outside their immediate community. They also encourage people to find their own coach if that's more appropriate. Coaches are encouraged to probe a deep exploration of what "God is brewing" by using the following three questions in each session.

Q. What is God brewing within you? (transformation)
Q. What is God brewing amongst you? (participation)
Q. What is God brewing around you? (contribution)

Practice Two: Action Reflection

Discipleship and disciple making are best forged in the everyday context of life. The ancient text of Deuteronomy said as much when it implored the Jewish people to wear their faith upon their hearts, to impress it on their children, to talk about it when they sit at home and when they walk along the road, when they lie down and when they get up.[27] In other words, they were to pass on their faith through the normal experiences of life, an action–reflection type process. They were to form their actions and thinking at the same time in the flow of life, instead of shaping their thinking hoping that new behavior would follow.

Again, this is how Jesus equipped the first disciples—it was on the road, in the hub of life, not in the temple. The world was Jesus's classroom. Our recommendation is to establish a practice of action–reflection within your community. It's simple to do; engage in discipleship and

Great Coaching Habits

Steve Ogne of CRM has been coaching church planters and training coaches for a number of years. He suggests the following seven habits for great coaching.[28]

- LISTEN for where God is working!
- CARE for personal needs!
- CELEBRATE what God is doing!
- STRATEGIZE for missional effectiveness!
- TRAIN in essential ministry skills!
- DISCIPLE the whole person!
- CHALLENGE specifically!

disciple making, then together reflect, pray, and establish theological frameworks. It's good to do this formally, as well as informally through everyday interactions.

Practice Three: Coaching

Coaching is one of the most important aspects in the discipleship process. It's an intentional relationship in which a coach seeks to empower, equip, and energize the individual to grow in Christlikeness. It seeks to empower the individual to evolve skillfully, theologically, and spiritually, to increase their discipleship and disciple-making capacity.

Coaching is largely an action–reflection process in which a coach guides an individual in setting goals and evaluating progress. The individual engages in discipleship and disciple making, and then together with the coach reflects on her experiences and development. The role of the coach is to guide the person through a process of critical reflection on his practice and spirituality—his strengths, weaknesses, opportunities, and threats. This approach allows the individual freedom to experiment and then reflect with her coach. This process should also stimulate imagination and help probe alternative perspectives and approaches.

- Provide a pool of coaches for your group, which may mean finding and training them.

- Coaches don't necessarily need to be from your community. In fact, there are many benefits in having a coach from outside your immediate context.

- The best coaches are those who are attentive, who ask great questions and listen well. Great coaches know how to guide a person in establishing goals, evaluating those goals, and then helping to state them clearly in a memorable way.

- Make it compulsory for all stakeholders and leaders to receive coaching once per month.

Group Processing

Session 1: *Explore: (talk about it)*

- If you had to highlight one idea from this section, what would it be? Why?

- In your own words, explain discipleship and disciple making to another person in the group. What ideas excite you? Concern you?   .

- What are the best habits and practices to consider? We have provided a few. Can you think of any others?

- What questions do you have?

- How can you imagine the group growing in this area?

Session 2: *Evaluate (reflect deeper)*

- Is discipleship and disciple making a strength or weakness for your group?

- Does the majority of the group understand and believe in this concept?

- How is commitment to these ideas already demonstrated in your group? Give examples.

- When was the community best at discipleship and disciple making? What were the contributing factors? What was happening at the time?

- In your opinion, what are the most important issues for discipleship and disciple making?

- What challenges are ahead? What are the barriers? Where do you anticipate resistance?

Session 3: *Employ (act on it)*

- What needs to happen during the next twelve months? What do you need to do that you're not currently doing?

- What will you need to let go of?

- What information and resources will you need? Who else needs to be involved?

- How will you know if you have grown in these areas? What will the key indicators be?

- What habits and practices will you seek to integrate during the next twelve months? List them here.

Action Plans

What are the first steps you will take to achieve these goals? Looking at your past, are they realistic?

What—Activity/Action	When—Date	Who—Leader/Participants
1.		
2.		
3.		
4.		

Session 4: *Personal Journal*

After processing much information, take some time to pray, listen, and respond to God. How is God prompting you, and how will you respond? Take time to record your impressions as well as insights from the group. Write a prayer expressing your desires to God. If appropriate, share your thoughts in the group, and then pray together.

- What am I sensing from God?

- What is my prayer?

4

The Missional-
Incarnational Impulse

In this chapter we will look at the *missional-incarnational impulse*, which is in effect the practical outworking of the missionary God who sends the church *outward* into the world and *deep* into culture and context. It draws its inspiration from the incarnation and is energized by the mission of God. The purpose of combining these words is to link two practices that in essence form one and the same action, to *seed* and *embed* the gospel in different groups, cultures, and societies. This is a significant key to apostolic genius!

Missional

We have come to see that mission is not merely an activity of the church. It is the result of God's initiative, rooted in his desire to restore and heal creation. Mission means "sending" and is the central biblical theme describing God's action in human history. This sending is embodied and lived out in the missional impulse. It is the *outward* movement rooted in God's mission that compels the church to reach a lost world.

The Forgotten Ways describes the mission of God as a "sneeze-like" influence that releases the outward flow of the movement of God like seeds in the wind. It is contrasted with the attractional church, where the seeds are put in ecclesial storehouses, effectively extinguishing the purpose they were made for. It is suggested that the attractional model focuses on church growth, which hinders the power of multiplication and makes it impossible to release a movement.

Incarnational

John 1:1–18 describes the incarnation of Jesus, when he took human form and moved into the neighborhood in an act of humble love the world had never known. The central thrust of the incarnation was that by becoming one of us, God was able to achieve redemption for the human race and radical identification with all that it means to be human.

If God's way of reaching his world was to incarnate himself in Jesus Christ, then our way of reaching the world should likewise be incarnational. We need to exercise a genuine identification with those we are trying to reach so that they may come to know God through Jesus. The following framework is an example of how Jesus relates to us through the incarnation and how we can relate incarnationally to others.

> *Presence*—Jesus was God in the flesh. This is a God who moved into the neighborhood and lived with humanity. The idea of presence highlights the role of relationships and close connection in mission. When we hang out as representatives of Jesus, people get the idea that God is interested in fostering a relationship with them.

> *Proximity*—Not only was God in Jesus fully present to humanity, he interacted directly with people from every level of society. He ate with Pharisees as well as tax collectors and prostitutes. If we follow in his footsteps we need to be directly and actively involved in the lives of the people we are seeking to reach. This involves both spontaneity and regularity in our friendships with those beyond the church.

Powerlessness—If we truly desire to act like Christ, we cannot rely on conventional forms of power and leadership to communicate the gospel. We must practice Jesus's model of servanthood and humility in our relationships with one another and the world.

Proclamation—The gospel invitation initiated in the ministry of Jesus remains alive and active today. A genuine incarnational approach requires that we are always ready to share the gospel story. We cannot take this aspect out of our mission and remain faithful to our calling.

By living incarnationally we not only model the pattern of humility set up in the incarnation, but we also create space for mission to take place in organic ways. Mission becomes something that fits seamlessly into the ordinary rhythms of life, friendships, and community. Incarnational ministry essentially means taking the church to people rather than bringing people to church.

The Combined Impulse

The missional-incarnational impulse is a two-in-one action operating together like scissor blades. The missional impulse relates to the outward movement of the church as a sent people, while the incarnational pulse refers to the embedding and deepening of the gospel. Together they result in both multiplication and transformation.

It is not hard to see that the reproductive capacities of church are directly linked to this impulse. The mission of God requires the seeding and reproduction of God's people in every culture and group of people. Each unit of church can be conceived as a pod of seeds, each church pregnant with other churches. By insisting people come to us and seeking to control the mission environment, we lock up the power of multiplication. It seems that we suppress the "sneeze" by holding back the impulse to sneeze in the first place. To frustrate this impulse is to block the church's innate reproductive capacity.

The missional-incarnational impulse requires that we embed the gospel and the gospel community in the fabric of the host community. We must develop churches that are both true to the gospel and relevant to the context it is seeking to evangelize—genuine Jesus communities that seek to become a functioning part of the existing culture while seeking to transform it.

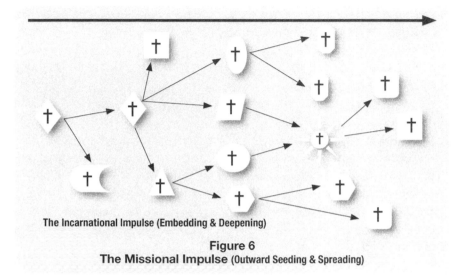

The Incarnational Impulse (Embedding & Deepening)

Figure 6
The Missional Impulse (Outward Seeding & Spreading)

Putting First Things First

To become a missional church, we must realign our priorities and recalibrate our approach to ministry. *Christology* determines *missiology*, and *missiology* in turn determines *ecclesiology*. What is meant here is that the person and work of Jesus must directly inform our purpose and function—our mission in the world. And it is our mission that in turn must inform the structure and cultural forms of the church. To align ourselves correctly, we first need to return our attention to Jesus Christ, the founder of Christianity, and recalibrate our approach from that point. Jesus is our constant reference point. When we go back to Jesus, we rediscover a whole new way of going about mission. From Jesus we learn to engage with people in an entirely fresh, "nonchurchy" way. He hung out with sinners and made the kingdom of God accessible and desirable to the average person.

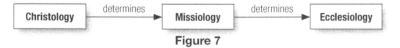

Figure 7

Church Follows Mission

The church is a dynamic expression of the people of God in any given place. Worship style, social dynamics, and liturgical expressions must result from the process of contextualizing the gospel in any given context. When we begin with incarnational mission, the church will explore its way of life and corporate expression within each cultural context. Thus, the church will be formed out of mission and missional action specific to its context. This is what is meant by *ecclesiology* following *mission*. In our cities and neighborhoods there are literally hundreds of different cultural subgroups that can be reached by such means.

Now let's explore a few examples of missional-incarnational practices used by churches around the world.

Suggested Habits and Practices

If we wish to embrace the missionary genius of the remarkable Jesus movements, we will need to recover a genuine missional-incarnational impulse as the primary posture and movement of God's people. God continues to send the church *outward* into the world as well as *deeper* into people's lives and contexts, to seed and embed the gospel. This *out* and *down* movement of the missional-incarnational impulse will provide the framework for us to explore its associated practices. Keep in mind that these two movements form one action and cannot exist without each other. Churches would do well to shape their way of life around this impulse.

We will look at the missional-incarnational impulse as two basic habits, each consisting of a number of suggested practices.

1. Going out
2. Going deep

Habit 1: Going Out

The "out" habit, and connected practices, is primarily focused on moving God's people out into the hub of life. A fellow missionary suggested that to sustain this outward impulse, a missionary group must incorporate proximity, frequency, and spontaneity into their collective life.[1] Let's explore these characteristics and how they relate to missional-incarnational practices.

Practice One: Proximity

This relates to the physical closeness Christians have with the people they are hoping to connect with. Jesus's commission to "go throughout the world" clearly indicates that the responsibility rests with the church to initiate this nearness and live each day in close proximity with those beyond the faith.[2] *Proximity* means that Christians need to be in direct proximity to the host community, rather than expecting the community to move toward them. Just as God through the incarnation moved into the neighborhood, the people of God should do likewise.

- Move into the neighborhood and live in close proximity to those with whom you wish to connect. That might mean that some members within your group choose to move house to actualize this closeness.

InnerCHANGE

As a mission order committed to sharing the good news among low socio-economic communities, InnerCHANGE began when John Hayes realized that driving *down to* and *moving into* poor neighborhoods were two very different propositions. He said that for too long he had been driving in and out of people's lives, so he found an apartment and moved into the neighborhood—Minnie Street, Santa Ana, Orange County, California, to be precise. After many years of mission on Minnie Street, John, with his wife, Deanna, and daughter Savannah, relocated to inner-city San Francisco, where they lived and worked among locals. From there, they moved to the UK, where they continue their mission in close proximity to inner-city Londoners. A collective commitment all InnerCHANGE workers make is to spend 80 percent of their time in the local neighborhood—an impressive commitment to proximity!

- Discover where locals gather and connect, and locate the mission group within these social hubs. It's a good idea to become part of these local rhythms and, as a group, to regularly spend time in these places. Spend time in third places,[3] such as local cafés or sports clubs. Through frequenting these establishments, you will also develop connections with the staff, owners, and other patrons. Maybe you can meet your friends or work colleagues on a regular basis for a drink or meal. This is a great context in which to introduce people from different social groups, like your soccer friends to your church friends.

- Hold some of your planning meetings in third places. Meet with your team and colleagues in local third places, rather than in a meeting room. Many of TPC's team meetings were held in their local pub. They found it was far more helpful planning and dreaming about their mission immersed within the actual mission context rather than removed from it. Try it. If it doesn't work, you can always go back to a meeting room.

- Walk your dog regularly. When Alan lived in Melbourne, Australia, he regularly took Ruby, his beloved boxer, for a walk throughout his local area and subsequently developed a number of relationships with other dog owners. They would stop and chat while their dogs played and sniffed one another. Just think—if you walked your dog a few times per week and regularly connected with the same people, over a year that's a significant amount of time in conversation with other community members.

- Rather than reading your book or writing your paper in the seclusion of your home or office, why not venture down to the local café, or library and do it

Hot Dogma

A group of missional Episcopalians in Pittsburgh decided to create this kind of proximity through the creation of a third place in the basement of their local cathedral. They developed a distinctive style of hot dog, arranged lounge chairs around the space, and scattered puzzles, games, and magazines on the tables. They serve great coffee and call the business Franktuary (originally, "Hot Dogma"). Their slogan we find wonderfully liturgical: "Franks be to God!"

Upstream Communities

This missional band in Western Australia made this move when five families sold their homes and relocated to Brighton, a new suburban development one hour north of Perth. For these families, among other changes, it meant selling their homes, locating new homes, securing employment, and enrolling the children in new schools. We find this a gutsy and smart way to enact proximity in mission.

there? Who knows? You might connect with someone and find more inspiration for your task.

• Join a community or interest-based group. Many Christians we've talked with tell us about the groups they've joined in the hope of connecting with others. Book clubs, Amnesty International, sporting groups, fitness classes, belly dancing, parents groups, and community garden co-ops are just some of the groups we've heard about. Check out what's in your area; we bet there are heaps to choose from.

• Find a hobby. If you have one, great. If you don't, find a hobby and connect with others who share a similar passion.

Practice Two: Frequency

Frequency pertains to the regularity of this connection. Proximity locates the Christian community among people, but frequency builds the familiarity needed for authentic relationships and community to

Phil and Laina

Christian Associates missionaries Phil and Laina Graf live with their five children in the heart of Amsterdam. To develop genuine connection with the locals, Phil and Laina frequently venture down to a local jazz club for a meal and to enjoy some of the finest live music. Through this regularity, they have become close friends with the club owner and local musicians, as well as many other patrons. Via these connections they have now been introduced to many others in the area. This is smart mission thinking and practice. They not only have identified where people are gathering but regularly locate themselves in the heart of this social activity.

develop. It's one thing to identify with the locals; it's quite another to be identified as the locals. Frequency is the key.

- Adopt a local watering hole or equivalent. It might be a café, the beach, or a certain park in your area. Obviously, it will be different for every context. Identify a local place in harmony with your group focus, and hang out there regularly. The key is to move from identifying with the locals to *actually becoming one*. This is exactly what Jesus did through the incarnation.

- Shop at the same places. Historically, the marketplace was a hub for meaningful connection. We need to recover the marketplace as a setting for connecting with others and building community. Try to purchase your food and household items at the same store every time. Whether that's the local butcher, grocer, fishmonger, supermarket, or hardware store. Don't chase the bargains but commit to supporting your local shopkeepers and producers. You'll develop familiarity not only with the staff and owners, but also with the

The Joshua Tree

The group Joshua Tree in Queensland, Australia, gathers most Sunday mornings for breakfast down at the local beach. They fire up the barbeque, cook their eggs and bacon, and spend the morning hours eating and talking. After breakfast some go for a swim or surf, or simply chat as they relax on the grass next to the beach. Instead of inviting families to a church service, the JT members simply invite their friends to the beach for breakfast. What a great way to spend Sunday morning, but more importantly, it's a healthy way to develop familiarity with others.

other customers. Imagine if everyone in your mission group did this! Enjoy your shopping, and view it as a great opportunity for mission.

- Spend time at the school fence. Organize your day so that when you pick up your children from school, you can spend a little more time chatting with the other parents. There's always at least one parent or teacher ready to chat. Maybe you could invite them back to your home for a cup of coffee while your children play in the yard, or go for a walk to the local park together.

- In partnership with others in your mission group, invite people to your home for dinner or barbeque. Or venture out for a picnic or Sunday lunch at a café. If you do this on a biweekly basis with a reasonably small group of people, you will be able to develop significant relationships over the course of the year.

- Go out for lunch or coffee with work colleagues once a week. It's amazing how different the conversation becomes outside the immediate work context.

Practice Three: Spontaneity

While proximity locates Christians among people, and frequency develops the familiarity required for relationships, spontaneity provides the flexible environment needed to grow deeper connections. Genuine relationships develop informally through unplanned and impromptu connections. But, by definition, *spontaneity* doesn't occur without making space for it. Missionary groups have to prepare for it by creating space in their life and mission. Churches desiring to engage people in mission will need to make sure they are not too busy to welcome the unexpected.

- Implant deep within the mission group a flexibility and openness to spontaneity. Expect that as a result of proximity and frequency, opportunities for spontaneity will arise. Clever mission groups anticipate spontaneity and realize it is crucial to be adaptable and responsive.

- Make room for people. This will mean evaluating how you currently spend your time individually and as a group. In light of this, reorder your individual and collective life to include spontaneity with others. If we are honest, most of us will see that we are too busy for meaningful connection. We must slow our pace, as nothing can be loved at speed.

- Free up your weekends. Many in the West still enjoy their leisure time on weekends, so make sure you keep enough spare time to socialize on Saturday and Sunday. For many people, Saturdays are taken up with catching up on sleep, sports, grocery shopping, cleaning the house, and the like. Sunday is increasingly the time when people, and in particular families, have their leisure time together. So free up your time to connect on weekends. By the way, guess where most Christians are on Sundays?

- Streamline the organization and administration requirements for your group. Limit the time and energy needed to keep the machine running. If your mission group or church is an incorporated entity, there are obvious legal requirements and processes you need to adhere to, such as banking, reporting, and insurance. But keep it as minimal as possible.

- Simplify the way your church learns and gathers. Organize communal gatherings and worship times in a way that minimizes the time and energy of church members. Arrange your church gatherings around the lifestyles and schedules of the host community. If the people you are connecting with are out and about socializing on

Questions for Reflection on Proximity, Frequency, and Spontaneity

Here are a few questions each missionary group can ask and reflect upon periodically. This will help the group assess whether they are embracing the mission potential of proximity, frequency, and spontaneity.

- Q. Are we in close proximity with those we feel called to? Give example of proximity.
- Q. Are we spending regular time with these people? Give example of frequency.
- Q. Are we too busy to develop meaningful relationships? Give example of spontaneity.

a Sunday morning or afternoon, then hold your church meetings at another time, so you can spend time with them.

- Limit the frequency of your in-house gatherings. How often does a congregation need to meet? Some mission groups we know have decided to meet three to four times per calendar month in order to release their time for missional engagement. These churches have remarked that as a result, they have experienced a higher percentage of attendance at their gatherings, and that fellowship has grown stronger as people have time to engage in mission together. If you want to foster fellowship and build community spirit, then engage in mission and service together. People will coalesce far more profoundly when they are involved in activity beyond themselves.

- Limit planning meetings. Establish how often you need to meet for planning, and stick to it. If you want to spend more time together as a team for developing camaraderie, then engage in mission together. This will build far more solidarity that sitting around planning mission.

Spontaneity is about having the time to sit down for a coffee and chat with someone who visits unexpectedly, or feeling free to stop and talk with a person you've bumped into on the street. Or it can simply be inviting people to your house for dinner on the spur of the moment. On a broader level, it's feeling free to abandon programs and strategies if they obstruct meaningful connection with others.

Embracing proximity, frequency, and spontaneity is nothing less than integrating mission into the natural rhythms of everyday life. Rather than seeing mission as a compartment or program, view it seamlessly as a way of life. We highly recommend that mission groups guide their individual and collective lives to connect with the lifestyles of those they wish to serve.

Practice Four: Ask Missionary Questions

In positioning a missional group in the appropriate places within the community, it is important to ask a series of missionary-type questions. We cannot highlight enough the value of this practice. Here are a few samples of the kind of questions that need to be asked.

- Where are people gathering and experiencing community?
- Where are people finding meaning and a sense of identity?
- What are the current existential issues? Where are people expressing a longing for the divine?
- How does the gospel address these issues? What is "good news" for these people?
- Where is God already at work in the community? And how can we join with God?
- Given the above answers, what will church look like for this community?

Once a group has reflected on these questions, it will be in a better position to ask the following question.

- Who is it that God has called us to? Who are the people with whom we desire to build meaningful relationships? Is it the surfing culture, young families, senior citizens, people who socialize in third places, or those who reside in a particular geographical area? In today's climate of diversity and complexity, strategically minded mission groups will focus on a host culture and aim to weave their lives into the very fabric of that community.

Practice Five: Find People of Peace

Authentic organic mission will mean being introduced to the host community through its existing members. Therefore, in the early stages it is essential to befriend local leaders and influencers as a natural introduction to that community. Quoting Luke 10, Alan, in a previous book, referred to these people as "people of peace."[4] In that account, Jesus sent out seventy-two disciples ahead of him into every place he was planning to visit. Jesus instructed them to find a "person of peace" in each area, to stay in their homes, and to eat and drink with these hosts as an organic way into that community. We assume from the basis of that relationship that the host would then introduce his guests to his neighbors and other acquaintances, providing the connection for the disciples to introduce Jesus. People of peace are influential members of the community who have good reputations and are spiritually open.

Locating these people and spending time developing meaningful connections will be a key step in the process of seeding and embedding the
gospel in every new context.

Habit 2: Going Deep

The "deepening" habit and its related practices are concerned with implanting the gospel in a local context through meaningful relationships.
It seeks to move the Christian community deep into culture and life.[5]
Whereas the missional impulse requires time and is crucial, as it sends
God's people into the hub of life, it is only the beginning of a genuinely
biblical form of mission. The incarnational impulse, with its attentiveness
to context, must lead followers of Jesus deeper into the lives of the people
they are seeking to reach. Whereas the goal of the missional impulse is to
continually locate God's people among the host community where they
can lovingly share and incarnate the gospel, the incarnational impulse
seeks to *identify* with the host community, *reveal* God's character and
presence, and *redeem* through embedding the gospel.

Practice One: Meaningful Engagement

To implant the gospel in any given context, it is necessary to create
an environment where the mission group enjoys ongoing meaningful
engagement with its host community. We are surprised how daunted
many Christians are at the prospect of this level of engagement with
those outside the religious community. Sadly, we believe the Christian
community has largely forgotten the importance and the art of building
friendships with those beyond the church. Ironically, this is what Jesus
was so good at! The missional community is called to bring meaning
and spiritual reflection into everyday life, because that is precisely where
people engage. To do this, we will have to remember and relearn how
to engage meaningfully. A litmus test for this is to periodically ask, "Are
we a significant part of other people's lives? Do these people think that
we add meaning and value to their lives?"

- Allow the natural process of relationship development to take its
  course. Genuine relationships require time and commitment. We
  cannot fast-track relationships. Allow for time and space.

- Engage in culture and view it as an asset, not a threat. Read books that are not by Christian authors, both fiction and nonfiction. Regularly read the newspaper or explore current affairs online. Go to the movies. And so on. How can we meaningfully connect with others if we are not engaging in the same world? It is impossible to wholly interpret culture from the outside. This is largely a prophetic role, so seek out the prophets in your midst and follow their lead.

- Rites of passage such as weddings, funerals, birthdays, birth celebrations, and the like are profound contexts in which to build meaningful connection. Sadly, fewer people seek the church to conduct these ceremonies. This is missionary ground we need to recover. Sharing these deeply meaningful rites of passage with others is a profound missional experience. It's a huge invitation into their world. Giving meaning to life's transitions is one of the roles the church should play best. In this way, missional groups could provide meaningful celebrations for those who ask, and serve as a type of chaplain to the host community. Often the process of planning together will provide just as much meaningful connection as the celebration itself. Keep in mind that in today's climate, people welcome meaningful celebrations with open arms but, in general, are not interested in a particularly "religious" ceremony. It's important that missionary groups are flexible and adaptive.

- Recover the art of conversation. Look to the Gospels, and notice how Jesus interacts with people, the questions he asks, and the replies he gives. He was a master conversationalist. Mission communities would do well to learn how to conduct meaningful conversations by developing their listening and interpersonal skills. If you're privileged to have social workers in your community, ask them to enhance the group's capacity to interact and converse through developing and learning new skills.

- Be intentional beyond the social moments. It's very important that we attend relationships outside of the general social times. It's not enough to be a good conversationalist at a party or the pub. You must follow up with people to develop a meaningful relationship. So make that phone call and invite them out for coffee, or invite them over for dinner, or send them that encouraging text message.

- Build relational networks. Rather than developing programs or religious spaces, seek to create a network of significant friendships spread throughout the host community. Michael Frost has suggested that as we develop this system of relationships, more and more people from the community will be swept into this network. He likened this to the ancient process of fishing, where together people used nets, as opposed to a single person with a rod, hook, and line. He suggested that in the same way the first-century fishermen prepared their nets, we will need to spend significant time on building the network of friendships.[6] It might be helpful at some point to map the relationships across the mission group to highlight common patterns and connections as a way to discern how to best arrange your time.

- Spend the majority of your time with just a few. Unfortunately, we cannot befriend everyone within sight. Most of us have the capacity to build significant relationships with just a handful of people. This is a missionary discipline that many find harsh, but in the end it is actually more loving. Identify those people you feel led to spend more time with, and concentrate on these relationships as a priority.

- Share projects. In his book *The Shaping of Things to Come*, Alan suggested shared projects as a simple but profound way to build meaningful connection with those beyond the church.[7] Through working on useful endeavors shoulder to shoulder with those in the host community, significant conversation, shared values, and deep connection naturally develop. This is called camaraderie, and it will be explored in more depth in the *communitas* section. These projects might already exist within the community; or a mission group can easily start one and invite others to join. Here are a few ideas:

  * Join a cooperative that aims to clean up local areas or polluted waterways.
  * Start or join a local art group that installs art within public spaces.
  * Organize an awareness and fundraising initiative for a local nonprofit group or school.

* Initiate a community garden to grow fruits, herbs, and vegetables.
* Become a member of a local political group.

Practice Two: Proclamation

A genuine incarnational approach will require that missional groups are prepared to share the gospel story with those around them. While we recognize that the gospel message must always be embodied in the life of the church,[8] it's a responsibility and privilege for God's people to share the story of Jesus with those around them.

It's clear that the post-Christendom environment in which we live requires a new approach to evangelism. How this is embodied, we believe, is largely up to each group and particular context. The New Testament writers viewed evangelism as highly relational and casual, as they encouraged all believers to talk about Jesus through everyday interactions. Paul encourages us to make the most of every opportunity, to let our conversations be full of grace, seasoned with salt, in order to know how to answer everyone.[9] Peter similarly recommends that we should always be prepared to give an answer to those who ask us to the give reason for the hope we have. But, he adds, we are to do this with gentleness and respect.[10] Evangelism in this light will be more conversation, less presentation.

Alan has suggested the following framework for this kind of natural evangelism:[11]

* Excite curiosity through storytelling.
* Provoke a sense of wonder and awe.
* Be extraordinarily loving.
* Explore how God has touched their lives.
* Focus on Jesus.

In Psalm 139 David implies that before we were born we enjoyed a subconscious awareness of God—that he knew each of us within the womb. Jewish mysticism likewise proposes that each person is born with an experience and memory of God. It suggests that as we enter the world through birth, we forget this connection but, paradoxically, the same process results in our ability to remember. Could it be that evangelism is a process of helping people *remember* and *reconnect* with their maker? Maybe it's more helpful to view evangelism as *uncovering* the God who is *already present* in their lives. In this sense, evangelism would be focused on *evoking* the memory of God and would consist of *probing*, *prodding*, and asking insightful questions. The writer of Ecclesiastes similarly highlights that God has set eternity in each person's heart and that everyone at some point will yearn for connection with their Creator.[12]

Our task as missionaries, modeled squarely on Jesus, is to discern this movement of God in people's lives. We must revive the old Wesleyan doctrine of prevenient grace—the fact that God is deeply and profoundly at work in every person, calling them to himself through Jesus Christ.

- Begin with the assumption that God is not far from anyone.
- Ask questions like, "Have you had spiritual experiences?" or "When have you felt close to God?"
- Build on what people know and have experienced.
- Explore the gospel stories together.
- Share your own story.

Practice Three: Holy Living

While it is important that we proclaim the gospel through our words, it is equally important that we do so through our actions and lives. In a very real and tangible way, our lives are our messages and will either give integrity to what we say or undermine our words altogether. Jesus said, "let your light shine before men, that they may see your good deeds and praise your Father in heaven."[13] Likewise, Peter encouraged us to live such good lives among the broader community that they may see our good deeds and glorify God.[14] Paul echoed this sentiment when he wrote that our lives are to shine like stars in the universe.[15] How we live is integral to seeding and embedding the gospel.

The hope is that as we live holy lives, people will be intrigued and inspired to seek God. The only hitch is that Christianity has a reputation for suppressing life and its pleasures rather than embracing them. What has constituted "holy living" has done exactly the opposite and driven people away from God. A missional-incarnational response is to begin to redeem everyday life, its experiences and pleasures, as gifts from God that can in fact reveal qualities about the Creator. If we are to have any real impact in this era, we will need to give new expression to "holy living."

If you want an example, look no further than Jesus. He is the best reference point for holy living. The disciple Matthew highlighted that this holiness was of a different kind altogether when he quoted Jesus as saying, "The Son of Man came eating and drinking, and they say, 'Here is a glutton and a drunkard, a friend of tax collectors and 'sinners.'"[16] This is surely the kind of holy living we need to mirror. Jesus's love for life and people attracted many. He ate and drank and socialized with people regardless of their race, lifestyle, gender, or religion, and some in the religious community called him a drunkard for it. If we wish to communicate to those around us that God is gracious, hospitable, interesting, and celebrative, we had better embody these qualities collectively. You'll be surprised how many people notice.

It's straightforward and commonsense, but when life gets too busy we forget that holy living and proclamation fit together and should never exist apart.

Practice Four: Hospitality

The practice of hospitality is much broader than simply "putting on a good spread" for Sunday lunch. Essentially, hospitality is an expression and experience of God's character. It's more about what people sense and how they feel when they're in your midst. TPC in Hobart define their call to practice hospitality as *creating an environment where people in their local community experience the character of God, feel a sense of belonging before believing, and can explore their spirituality with freedom.*

- Shared meals. Simply eat regularly with those in your host community and recover the shared meal as fundamental to missionary engagement. Eating and drinking together exposes people to God's character enfleshed within community. It communicates that God is hospitable, welcoming, enriching, lavish, celebrative, indiscriminate, nourishing, interesting . . . the list goes on! The Gospels are filled with stories where Jesus is found at a table connecting over food and wine. To a group of missionaries longing to be shaped by the habits of Jesus, these stories are inspirational and defining. If we desire to re-enchant Westerners with Jesus, the meal table, along with other forms of celebrating, will play a central role as we follow Christ's lead and create environments of belonging before believing. It is undoubtedly one of the best modes for mission for the West.

- Share your table regularly with the poor. This in itself is one of the most profound ways to change the world and be changed ourselves. If every Christian family were to have a poor person over for a meal once a week, we would literally transform the world through eating.

- Recover the "art of partying." Christians are not generally known for hosting lively parties, and yet we are the ones who have profound reason to celebrate. If Jesus is anything to go by, he whipped up a little more of the good stuff at a wedding in Cana and turned a rather average party into a hoot! We should be the ones to host the best parties, where people really celebrate and enjoy life. There is something within the relaxed, celebrative vibe of a party, where there are food and drink and music, that people respond to and wish to engage at deeper levels.

Practice Five: Contextualizing Community

The deepening impulse of the incarnational mode must eventually express itself in the formation of a fully contextualized Christian community. By this we mean that over time a new faith community will emerge and begin to form its "way of life" in reference to its immediate context. This newly gathered community will need to cultivate an endemic spirituality that has meaningful resonance within its environment. They will also disciple new Christians within the same context, allowing them to follow Christ and remain in their own culture. A truly incarnational mode will also allow the natural lifestyle patterns of the host community to shape the church's life and worship. Incarnational mission works to integrate the gospel into the people group without damaging the innate cultural framework that gives that community history, purpose, and meaning. The gospel, therefore, will change and fashion the community from within.

This raises the question, "How will new faith communities be sustained?" What practices, disciplines, and rhythms will be incorporated to ensure rigorous discipleship and sustainability? What will these new churches look like? How will they gather or corporately connect with God, serve the community? These are questions each missionary group will need to explore together with members from the host community.

- Build church around people in *their* context. Remember that church flows out of mission and should be expressed within its cultural environment.
- Listen to the people. Minister as if you have a stethoscope pressed up against their world. Develop an increased attentiveness to the issues related to the given culture, and avoid assuming you know what good news is to them or what the church should look like in their culture.
- Spend more time listening to, eating with, and playing with the neighborhood you live in. Work toward not merely identifying with the locals; seek to become one.
- Critically examine the culture together with the locals. What values within the culture promote the gospel, and what obstructs it? How can we use the godly values within this context to point to Jesus? And how can we redeem the values and customs that lead away from Christ? Seek to redeem the existing culture and guide it to its destiny in God, rather than impose an alien model upon it. Carry the Bible in one hand and a cultural map in the other.
- Experiment with new symbols and rituals that give fresh expression to the Christian experience. Explore the host community's history and culture to find practices that will enrich the collective experience and expression. This exploration is best done together with new Christians.

For a detailed exploration into contextualization we recommend reading "The Contextualized Church," chapter 5 in *The Shaping of Things to Come*.[17]

Practice Six: Send

We have already noted that God continues to send the church outward into the world as well as deeper into culture. Mission groups would do well to imitate this process and continue to send small groups from within their community to seed and embed the gospel in new contexts. This will ensure the missional incarnational impulse is embedded deep within the missional community. In short, continue to move *out* and *down*.[18] Remember, the reproductive capacities of the church are directly linked to this impulse, as each unit of church can be understood as a pod filled with seeds, or pregnant with other churches.

Here is an example of a process that Darryn provided for the mission group he works with. This map was shaped in the context of mission while the initial group was going through the very process. Often the question was asked, "What next?" which led to discovering the next step. This is what they came up with. Since then, it has been refined and used again and again as groups are sent into new contexts.

Missional Impulse Out into the World			Incarnational Impulse Down into Culture and Life		
1 ➤	2 ➤	3 ➤	4 ➤	5 ➤	6
The Mission-ary God	Individual Dreaming	Collective Dreaming	Contextual Dreaming	Contextual Practices	Contextual Community
Mission begins with God's redemptive dream and activity for the world. God is the primary missionary who sent His son and calls his people to join him in his redemptive purposes.	The God of Mission connects with an individual and embeds deep in their mind, heart, and soul a calling to partner with the divine dream. Considering mission is a communal vocation & endeavor. The dream must be shared with others.	The dream is shared with others, who also share their God-inspired dreams. The dream is clarified, honed & enhanced in community. A missionary group and collective dream will emerge along with a shared missionary identity, core values, and minimum discipleship standard.	The individual dreams which have now been clarified, honed, and enhanced in community are localized for a particular context. The missionary group engages in cultural analysis and self-analysis to determine its inner strengths, weaknesses, and resources.	The group now establishes an intentional missionary presence in harmony with the contextual dream. Missional rhythms and practices suitable for the context are formed and lived. The gospel and host community interface with greater-than-before intent.	In time a new faith community will, hopefully, emerge from the group's missional presence. This new church starts the process of forming its way of life in reference to its context. Over time the contextual community will be well positioned to further reach its context.

PROXIMITY, FREQUENCY, SPONTANEITY

Intentionality, Meaningful Engagement, Gospel / Culture Interface, Corporate Expression

Group Processing

Session 1: *Explore (talk about it)*

- If you had to highlight one idea from this section, what would it be? Why?

- In your own words, explain the missional-incarnational impulse to another person in the group. What ideas excite you? Concern you?

- What are the best habits and practices to consider? We have provided a few. Can you think of any others?

- What questions do you have?

- How can you imagine the group growing in this area?

Session 2: *Evaluate (reflect deeper)*

- Is the missional-incarnational impulse a strength or a weakness for your group?

- Does the majority of the group understand and believe in this concept?

- How is commitment to these ideas already demonstrated in your group? Give examples.

- When was the missional-incarnational impulse most active in your community? What were the contributing factors? What was happening at the time?

- In your opinion, what are the most important issues for embracing a missional-incarnational impulse?

- What challenges are ahead? What are the barriers? Where do you anticipate resistance?

Session 3: *Employ (act on it)*

- What needs to happen during the next twelve months? What do you need to do that you're not currently doing?

- What will you need to let go of?

- What information and resources will you need? Who else needs to be involved?

- How will you know if you have grown in these areas? What will the key indicators be?

- What habits and practices will you seek to integrate during the next twelve months? List them here.

Action Plans

What are the first steps you will take to achieve these goals? Looking at your past, are they realistic?

What—Activity/Action	When—Date	Who—Leader/Participants
1.		
2.		
3.		
4.		

Session 4: *Personal Journal*

After processing much information, take some time to pray, listen, and respond to God. How is God prompting you, and how will you respond? Take time to record your impressions as well as insights from the group. Write a prayer expressing your desires to God. If appropriate, share your thoughts in the group, and then pray together.

- What am I sensing from God?

- What is my prayer?

5

Apostolic Environment

What kind of environment allows the elements of mDNA, or "Apostolic Genius," to flourish? What kind of environment released the spontaneous growth of the Chinese and the New Testament churches? In *The Forgotten Ways*, Alan suggested that this unique setting is known as an apostolic environment.

In every movement there is a powerful form of influence that weaves its way through the chaotic network of churches and believers. There is no other substantial word for this catalytic influence other than, to reinvoke biblical language, *apostolic*. Wherever and whenever the church has significantly extended the mission of God or experienced rapid growth, there has always been apostolic leadership present in some form or another.

The apostolic person's calling is essentially the extension of Christianity. As such, he or she calls the church to its essential calling and helps guide it to its destiny as a missionary people with a transformative message for the world. All other functions of the church must be qualified by its mission to extend the redemptive mission of God through its life and witness. The apostolic leader thus embodies, symbolizes, and *re*-presents the church's mission to the missional community. Furthermore, he or she calls forth and develops the gifts and callings of all of God's people.

Without apostolic ministry, the church either forgets its high calling or fails to implement it successfully. Sadly, in declining denominational systems, such people are commonly "frozen out" or exiled, because they disturb the equilibrium of a system in stasis. This loss of the apostolic influencer is one of the major reasons for mainstream denominational decline. If we really want missional church, then we must have a missional leadership system to drive it—it's that simple.

Two major challenges face us as we seek to appropriate apostolic ministry in the Western church. The first is confusion between the unique role and calling of the original apostles and that of present-day apostolic ministry. Many fail to see that contemporary apostolic ministry is a gifting that continues and enhances the original work of the New Testament apostles, particularly the Twelve. But apostolic ministry today does not alter the original apostolic ministry in the process. The net result of authentic apostolic ministry is the extension of Christianity through multiplication.

The second challenge is that many who claim apostolic gifting today do it an injustice and regularly discredit the role through the abuse of authority. The apostolic leadership dynamic that needs to be emphasized is that of servant-inspirer, not one who "lords it over others." It is more about spiritual authority than it is about organizational governance. Genuine apostolic ministry is authenticated by suffering and empowerment rather than by positional authority. It draws its authority from service and calling, from moral and spiritual influence.

The Apostolic Task

The essential role of the apostolic leader is to be a custodian of the DNA of God's people, or to say it another way, the custodian of the gospel. But when we ask what this means in practice, we can break down the role into three primary functions, namely:

1. **To embed mDNA through pioneering new ground for the gospel and the church.**
   The apostolic person is continually pioneering new missional initiatives and new churches to extend Christianity. This often involves cross-cultural work but is not limited to it. The apostolic

leader continues to implant all aspects of mDNA in each community that is formed.

2. **To guard mDNA through the application and integration of apostolic or missional theology.**

The apostolic leader makes sure that each church remains true to the gospel and its missional ethos. He or she acts to create a web of meaning that holds the movement together through sharing stories, developing organizational ethos, corrective teaching, and cultivating leaders. Having imparted the mDNA in the first place, they then work to ensure churches do not mutate into something other than God intended them to be.

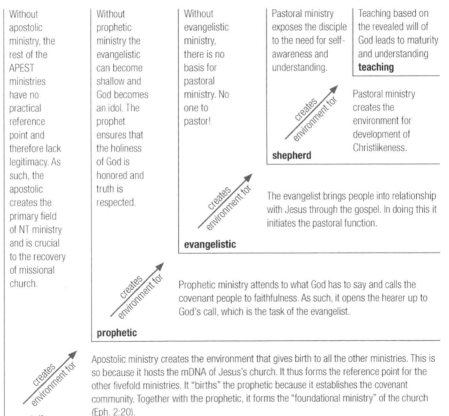

Without apostolic ministry, the rest of the APEST ministries have no practical reference point and therefore lack legitimacy. As such, the apostolic creates the primary field of NT ministry and is crucial to the recovery of missional church.

Without prophetic ministry the evangelistic can become shallow and God becomes an idol. The prophet ensures that the holiness of God is honored and truth is respected.

Without evangelistic ministry, there is no basis for pastoral ministry. No one to pastor!

Pastoral ministry exposes the disciple to the need for self-awareness and understanding.

Teaching based on the revealed will of God leads to maturity and understanding. **teaching**

Pastoral ministry creates the environment for development of Christlikeness.

creates environment for
shepherd

The evangelist brings people into relationship with Jesus through the gospel. In doing this it initiates the pastoral function.

creates environment for
evangelistic

Prophetic ministry attends to what God has to say and calls the covenant people to faithfulness. As such, it opens the hearer up to God's call, which is the task of the evangelist.

creates environment for
prophetic

creates environment for
apostolic

Apostolic ministry creates the environment that gives birth to all the other ministries. This is so because it hosts the mDNA of Jesus's church. It thus forms the reference point for the other fivefold ministries. It "births" the prophetic because it establishes the covenant community. Together with the prophetic, it forms the "foundational ministry" of the church (Eph. 2:20).

	Definition	Focus/core tasks	Impact when monopolizing
Apostolic	—essentially, the steward of the gospel and, therefore, the DNA of the church. As the "sent ones," apostolic ministry and leadership ensures that Christianity is faithfully transmitted from one context to another context and from one era to another.	—extending Christianity —guarding and embedding DNA of the church, both theologically and missionally —establish the church in new contexts —"founding" the other ministries (APEST) —development of leaders and leadership systems —maintain strategic missional perspective —trans-local networking	—tendency to autocratic styles of leadership, leaving many wounded people in the organization due to the task and future orientation of the apostle —lots of challenge and change, but not enough healthy transition, which requires the pastoral and teaching functions
Prophetic	—essentially, the person who is particularly attuned to God and his will. Therefore, speaks for God and calls the dominant consciousness to account.	—discerning and communicating God's will —ensuring the obedience of the covenant community —questioning the status quo	—one-dimensional, "hobby-horse" feel to things can lead to factiousness. —left to own devices, P types can be either overly activistic and driven or, paradoxically, passive and otherworldly
Evangelistic	—essentially, the recruiter to the cause, the infectious communicator of the gospel message. Calls for personal response to God's redemption in Jesus.	—making clear the offer of salvation so that people might hear and respond in faith —recruiting to the cause —church growth	—loss of overarching vision and purpose for the church based on narrow perspectives on faith and ecclesial life
Shepherding	—essentially, the shepherd who cares for and develops the people of God by leading, nurturing, protecting, and discipling them.	—cultivating a loving and spiritually mature network of relationships and community —making disciples	—closed, nonmissional, status quo community that cultivates a codependency between church and pastor (messiah complex) —can create an overly passive, "feminine" spirituality that can alienate males in the church
Teaching	—essentially, the ministry that clarifies the revealed mind/will of God so that the people of God gain wisdom and understanding	—discernment —guidance —helping the faith community to explore and seek to understand the mind of God —theologizing (developing the ideological component)	—theological dogmatism bordering on Christian gnosticism and a dry intellectualism —when controlling, can be dangerously ideological and pharisaical

3. To create an environment where other ministries emerge.
The apostolic gift creates the environment for the release and nurture of all other gifts listed in Ephesians 4. It is therefore the foundational gift that gives context to the prophetic, evangelistic, pastoral, and teaching gifts listed in Ephesians. This collection of gifts is identified as APEST. This role also creates the ecclesial fabric or network that is so important to a genuine movement ethos.

In some sense these three roles within the apostolic function can be likened to that of cultural architect, because they create the necessary environment and connections out of which the gospel can advance and the church can flourish. Note in the following diagram that the apostolic plays a foundational role from which the other gifts emerge

The APEST ministries of Ephesians 4 include apostolic, prophetic, evangelistic, pastoral, and teaching (or didactic). Each of these functions has an important and necessary role in the church. However, it has been noted that for the most part, the church has obscured the need for apostolic leadership. The system has weighted itself in favor of teaching and pastoral care, directly marginalizing the apostolic, prophetic, and evangelistic ministries. This has been disastrous for the church. To understand the different nature of each of the APEST ministries, we need to explore their core tasks, functions, and impacts as seen in the previous table.

It is also suggested that Ephesians 4:7,11–12 assigns the APEST ministries to the entire body, and not just the leaders, as all believers have these callings within them. Furthermore, each of these ministries draws on a variety of related gifts, as the whole system operates best together. For further reflection and insights regarding apostolic environment, please see chapter 6 in *The Forgotten Ways* and Alan's book *Primal Fire* (with Neil Cole and Wolfgang Simson, available fall 2009), which will thoroughly explore Ephesians 4 based ministry.

Now let us consider a few suggested habits and practices to create environments where missional churches flourish and multiply.

Suggested Habits and Practices

In approaching the practicalities of creating an apostolic environment, remember the three key functions of apostolic ministry: *to embed mDNA through pioneering new ground for the gospel, to guard mDNA through apostolic theology,* and *to create the environment for other ministries to emerge.* Considering these overarching apostolic functions, we suggest the following five habits and related practices.

1. Pioneer and multiply
2. Cultivate Apostolic Genius
3. Foster community calling and uniqueness
4. Develop ministry capacity
5. Catalyze

Habit 1: Pioneer and Multiply

Seeing that the apostolic calling is essentially about pioneering and multiplying Christianity, it's best to start with this as a habit in and of itself. This habit is located at the very heart of apostolic ministry. Nothing will establish a culture of pioneering and multiplication more than simply doing it. Easier said than done, we know! Here are a few practices to get you on your way.[1]

Practice One: New Initiatives

Regularly initiate new missionary incentives and communities. Many missional churches make a commitment to multiply their communities every twelve months. While we don't want to suggest such a rigid time-frame for reproduction, we do wish to highlight this type of commitment as very healthy. This kind of practice will ensure that an apostolic ethos is integrated into the ministry culture. Always have something new that you're dreaming and praying about together, training a team for, or taking the first steps toward. If you do this, over time pioneering and multiplying will become central to your collective identity.

Practice Two: Prepare New Missionary Teams

To regularly start these incentives, new missionary teams need to be identified and developed. The apostolic role in this situation is to stimulate and guide this process but not to control or micromanage it. It is an empowering function that seeks to stir imagination and create a setting for team development and self-organization. This process takes time; to hurry is counterproductive. People need space to dream together and form camaraderie. If you don't commit to this up front, it is doubtful you will ever get around to it, as other ministry issues crowd out the missional ones. Grassroots leadership and team development are strategic activities; don't leave them to chance.

Savvy missionary communities are continually preparing groups for new mission. In fact, each core unit of church (e.g., a cell group) within an existing community should be preparing for new mission and, in time, reproduce itself. For an example of the process for initiating new mission, see the chart on page 108 in chapter 4.

Practice Three: Experiment like Mad

As Oswald Sanders said, "A great deal more failure is the result of an excess of caution than of bold experimentation with new ideas. The frontiers of the Kingdom of God were never advanced by men and women of caution." We say, just give it a go. At the heart of pioneering mission is a willingness to take risks. If it doesn't work, you've just found another way not to do it, and everyone involved will have acquired new skills along the way.

Organic systems have trial and error built within their very nature. Bearing in mind that every context is different, there cannot be a one-size-fits-all approach, so experimentation is an essential practice if we want to find new ways to implant the gospel.

- Create a culture of permission to dream and try new things. Apostolic ministry exists to stir and awaken the missionary purpose of God's people. So go for it, dream, and experiment like mad!
- Reflect as a church on the pioneering nature of Christianity throughout history.
- Recall the inspiring examples of pioneering effort within scripture.
- Create real-life action heroes. It is critical that people are actually attempting to do what is being discussed and learned. Inspire a genuine pioneering spirit where innovators and other brave souls are encouraged and supported.

Practice Four: Implant a Multiplication Ethos from the Beginning

Integrate into the very fabric of the community a sustained commitment to multiplication. The Chinese church did this through the saying, "Every person a church planter, every church a church-planting church." What a great motto to arouse a multiplication philosophy! Implant within the heart of your community a "go forth and multiply" ethos. In our experience, many churches will resist this, so leadership will need to work hard at getting community buy-in and commitment to multiply. (This theme is further developed in the chapter 6.)

- Recount the stories of amazing multiplication, like the early church and the church in China.
- Encourage the entire community to read books like *The Starfish and the Spider*[2] and *The Tipping Point*.[3]
- Plant a seed by asking, "How can we make church as simple and reproducible as possible?" This is a question that's bound to stimulate a multiplication ethos along with numerous insightful ideas for the way ahead.

Practice Five: Provide a Framework to Dream and Plan

In establishing an apostolic environment, the group needs a map to guide their dreaming and planning. These maps can take the form of a step-by-step process to guide the team in detailed preparation, or helpful theological concepts and language that provide a meaningful framework for planning. Sometimes these maps can be established beforehand, but in reality most of them will emerge "just in time," or even in hindsight. This is helpful, as it will provide learning for future dreaming and planning. For an example of a framework that Darryn provided for the mission team he works with see page 108 in chapter 4.

Habit 2: Cultivate Apostolic Genius

To cultivate an Apostolic Genius ethos, an appropriate *culture* and *way of life* need to be fashioned. We know that culture is predominantly shaped by the daily *conversations*, *interactions*, and *practices* of the group's members. It follows, then, that to cultivate an Apostolic Genius culture, we need to ensure the group's *practices*, *interactions*, and *conversations* are of an apostolic nature.[4] While all this sounds potentially complex, the practices are reasonably straightforward.

Practice One: Develop an Understanding of the Apostolic Genius Model

The first practice we suggest in cultivating an Apostolic Genius ethos is to develop the group's understanding of the Apostolic Genius framework. Here are some ways we propose you can begin to do this.

- Get as many people to read *The Forgotten Ways* text as possible.
  We know that this is a comprehensive text containing complex terminology and many new paradigm shifts in how we think about church and movements. The reason for this detail is to dislodge our thinking from the current forms that exercise a monopoly over our imaginations. It's crucial we engage our minds and hearts in the quest to recover the forgotten ways of apostolic movements.
- Develop an understanding of change process.
  This is a significant role, particularly for leaders in established churches and organizations. It's our belief that an established church can change and become missional, but leaders will need to have a clear perspective on the change process required to get this done. Don't look for short-term solutions when the issues you deal with are complex.
- Embed Apostolic Genius at the core of the group.
  In cultivating Apostolic Genius it's helpful to implant the idea at the very heart of the group. If you're a new church planter you can lay down this as the base DNA and get it right from the start. To do that you'll need to make sure each of the members of your core team grapples with the ideas of Apostolic Genius. Much depends on what you build into the "stem cells" of the church. It is much better to get it right in the beginning. For those in established churches, you will need to work hard to dislodge the inherited imagination where it blocks Apostolic Genius.

- Think systems.

  The Forgotten Ways provides us with a way of seeing movements in their wholeness. It is not a one-dimensional look at the characteristics of movements; rather, it describes an entire system of interconnected elements. Because Apostolic Genius is a system, it is critical that you keep your eye on the whole while focusing on any of the singular elements. Never lose sight of the fact that a true apostolic movement needs all six elements to flourish.

Practice Two: Common Missional Practices

Essentially, missional practices are *a set of agreed-upon practical commitments* that guide a group in living out their dreams, identity, and values in ways consistent with their unique calling from God. Revisit the missional-incarnational impulse chapter (chapter 4) and outcomes from your conversations, as these will provide you with material to develop common, and sustainable, missional practices.

Fostering a set of common practices and way of life is an excellent way to act together as a missionary people, thus cultivating a robust apostolic consciousness in the process. This is why we suggest that all groups would benefit from forming a set of practices as a way to engage in mission in a collective and sustainable manner. In the process this will shift mission from a programmed activity to a common lifestyle which is vital for sustainability. Practices also move a group's values from preferred to actual and gives everyone in the community a clear framework of how they can contribute. We think you'll be surprised at how powerful this simple but profound practice can be.

The apostolic task here is to

- Educate the group about the importance of common practices.
- Guide the collaborative process in developing them.
- Provide a context for accountability.
- Ensure the practices are connected with their unique calling.

For examples of collective missional practices, see the resource section at the end of this book.

Practice Three: Theological Reflection

As a group reflects on how God works through his people across time to bring about his new creation, the community will be able to find itself as part of this unfolding redemptive story. It's crucially important that as God's people we read and explore scripture in this way as a living text. And even though the canon of scripture closed with Revelation, salvation history rolls on, and we can participate in it!

The continuous communication and discussion of mission-shaped theology should be done in many ways and in many contexts, both formally and informally. Just think creatively, and your community will come up with a host of ways to engage scripture.

Go to conferences together, get insightful talks on DVD, share important books and articles around the community, or invite a well-weathered incarnational practitioner to reflect on his or her missionary theology with your group. Set up the environment, and facilitate conversation around these themes. This process will shape and maintain the web of meaning that holds your mission community together. It will also offer your group new language and metaphors, as well as increased motivation.

For example, it is a requirement for all Third Place Communities stakeholders to attend at least one mission-related seminar annually and to read at least one missionary-themed book. Often the community will attend a conference together en masse. This has proven to be a helpful process in reflecting theologically together.

Practice Four: Retell Your Stories

The stories of our past formed who we are, and the stories we recall each day continue to shape us. Retelling your stories is unquestionably one of the most constructive practices a community can adopt. This is how you explain your calling and mission to yourself as well as to new members. Listening to one another retell stories from our experiences is how you step back and view your mission from afar. Remembering your stories will also allow you to discern where God has worked through you in the past. This will bring clarity for your future and remind you of your calling as a community.

Stories are inspiring. They provide energy, which often leads to action simply because it locates principle right in the heart of reality.

Stories connect because they demand attention. People can easily find themselves within a story, which in turn allows possibility: "If God used Jeremy to do that, maybe he can use me as well?"

We know of a missional community that hosts an annual dinner where they eat together and remember the stories of the past twelve months. This community also organizes a yearly weekend retreat for anyone interested in dreaming up the future. A significant portion of this weekend is spent recalling the stories of how and why they formed in the beginning.

A wise missional community will mine and treasure its stories. Here are a few ideas to get you started.

- Starting with the leadership team, make a commitment to remember and retell your stories as each member intermingles with others in the church group.
- Ask people for their cherished memories of engaging in mission together.
- Create slide shows. A picture paints a thousand words! Obviously, you will need photos for this, so document your ministry with a camera. Take photos of all the people with whom you are connecting, and of the places you connect, the parties, the food, the celebrations.
- Interview members for your newsletter. Ask them to talk about their favorite memories; get them to recall a story or two.
- Together, map how relationships began and developed. When did we meet John? Who met him first? How did it happen? Whom did he connect with next? Recall significant moments in your relationships.
- A simple question like, "How has God used us in the past?" will lead to many interesting stories.
- Get someone to write a book that collects the stories of the community and retells them in a compelling manner.

Practice Five: Action–Reflection

Establish a practice of action–reflection within the missional community. When you engage in mission together, make sure you put time aside to reflect and pray about it. It's beneficial to do this through a formal process, as well as informally through the everyday conversations among the group's members. Leaders will need to instigate and model the informal process themselves by incorporating reflection into the conversations they have with others in the community. Simply asking a fellow missionary how your shared mission of catching up with friends every week is going will do the trick. The informal practice is clear-cut: engage in mission, and then reflect and pray together.

It is important periodically to set aside a few days to reflect on the overall ministry direction and effectiveness. Weekend retreats are a great way to do this. A simple SWOT [5] analysis can be helpful here. There are numerous other evaluation tools and programs available, so do a little research, and choose (or create) the one that best suits your context.

Practice Six: Preserve Mission as the Organizing Principle

Part of the apostolic function is to create a missional organizational culture and then seek to ensure that the community remains true to it. Even for the most committed, action-oriented mission groups, the tendency will be to move away from mission and to become more inward-focused. As we have just mentioned under theological reflection, facilitating conversation around core missional theology will create the organizational culture and maintain the web of meaning and core purpose that holds the group together. It's a habit any group committed to missional church cannot afford to overlook.

Find ways to reawaken people to the gospel. One way Darryn has sought to do this in his community is through exploring distinct biblical themes that relate to the mission of God and the church. Take, for instance, the theme of *shalom*. The group has surveyed the subject through scripture, talked about it, dreamed of what it might look like in specific situations and contexts. This has also invigorated the group's commitment to evangelism by providing them with new language and images in talking with those not of the faith about the gospel.

A simple question you can ask to help preserve mDNA is, "Are we moving away from our primary calling as a missional people?" If yes, you can ask further questions, such as "How?" and "Why?" and "What do we need to do in order to realign with our core purpose?" More often than not, the reason that people have moved away from their primary calling is busyness. In that case, the apostolic role is to seek ways to help integrate mission into the everyday rhythms of life. This way, as long as people are living, they will be engaging in mission. This is preserving the missional DNA in theory and in action.

Practice Seven: Prayer

Regular mission-focused prayer is a valuable practice in the task of implanting Apostolic Genius. What a community talks to God about powerfully shapes its ethos. Corporate prayer is an essential part of a community's conversation and contributes to its culture, so keep mission at the fore of what you talk to God about when you are together. Prayer, among many benefits, directs our gaze toward God, the chief seeker of humanity. Collective prayer helps us listen together to God and teaches us to be attentive to his movements. Bill Hybels was right: we need to be seeker-sensitive, and prayer helps us to be so—sensitive to God, the ultimate seeker. Through regular mission-centered prayer, the community will be reminded that God is the source and energizer of mission.

The New Testament teaches us to pray for more evangelists, for a blessing on evangelistic activity, and for the salvation of those in our midst. Here are a few ideas you may wish to implement, but be creative and develop your own collective prayer habits.

- Organize prayer walks around areas in which you spend time connecting with people.
- Host prayer meetings specifically to pray for those with whom you are connecting.
- Encourage each member to pray every day for the church's mission and for the people with whom they are connecting.

Habit 3: Foster Community Calling and Uniqueness

In creating an apostolic environment, it is beneficial for a group to harness their missionary *identity* and *uniqueness*. Remember that apostolic ministry calls forth the common *identity* and *vocation* of God's people. Identity clearly relates to *who* a group is and its sense of *purpose*. A community's *uniqueness* is directly related. It refers to the specific *gift-ing* and *ability* God invests in a particular group of his people. As these themes are intimately related, we will deal with them together.

Some have referred to this specific gifting as the group "charism," taken from the Greek word *charis*, meaning "gift" or "grace." We prefer the term *uniqueness* and will use that from here on. A group's uniqueness, therefore, is the distinctive gifting God invests in a group of people. This communal gift is not a theological statement, but a deep-seated passion and intuition of why this group was called into being and the unique contribution they make to God's mission. Once discovered, a group's uniqueness will generate a clearer indication of a group's identity and calling. Ashley Barker recommends that connecting with the reasons God brought a specific community into being helps current and future workers find the passion, purpose, and contributions they can make collectively.[6] Apostolic leadership fosters the group's identity and uniqueness and endeavors to align its way of life to match. A simple way to do this is to carefully consider your uniqueness when forming your collective practices.

Discover Your Uniqueness

Instigate a process to discern your group's identity and uniqueness. How can a group do that? The answer is straightforward, but the pro-

---

Urban Neighbors of Hope (UNOH)

UNOH, a mission order among the poor, was inspired to take its founding experiences seriously. Ten years after UNOH formed, it embarked on a year-long journey to look deeper into where God had given its members passion and used them in the past. What they discovered was their founding uniqueness, simply stated, "to seek God's reign among the lost and poor incarnationally, and to help urban neighbourhoods facing poverty become like Christ-centred villages."[7] At the end of the process, the UNOH founders concluded that by focusing on these questions they were touching afresh why God brought them into being and in the process were identifying, nurturing and valuing their founding uniqueness.[8]

Third Place Communities

TPC discovered their uniqueness was simply to be *a missionary community within local third places*. Their deep-seated intuition of why God called them into being was to locate themselves within third-place culture, engage in the social rhythms, and practice the presence of Christ. They identified their unique contribution as participation within this culture, a place where few Christians ventured with missionary intent. They communicate their uniqueness as "a mission of hospitality in third and first places."[9] They describe hospitality as creating an environment where people experience the character of God, where people feel they belong before they believe, and a context in which to explore their spirituality with freedom and creativity.

cess requires patience and commitment. The way a group discovers its identity and uniqueness is simply through prayer and collaboration.

The importance of prayer can never be overstated. After all, the group's uniqueness has been given by God, so asking how he has distinctively graced your group is more than a good idea—it's crucial. So pray about it regularly.

By reflecting and collaborating on a series of insightful questions, the group will see their identity and gifting with more clarity. It's essential to recruit others outside the group who know the mission well to also reflect on the following questions. A balanced discernment process always includes wise and caring individuals who observe from a distance. Here is a list of questions that will help your group through this discernment process. Make sure you spend time on this; if you rush, you'll just have to do it again.

- Why did God bring this group into being in the first place?
- What were the founding passions and dreams?
- How has God worked through this group in the past?
- What are the group's current passions and dreams?
- What's the one thing this group does really well?
- What unique contribution does this group make to the broader mission of God?

Habit 4: Develop Ministry Capacity

In growing an apostolic environment, the community's capacity for ministry must be continually increased. Apostolic influence develops the group's ministry aptitude and fitness primarily through calling forth and developing the gifts, passions, and skills of God's people. The best way to do this is to broaden the ministry base to include the fivefold forms of ministry outlined in Ephesians 4: apostles, prophets, evangelists, shepherds, and teachers—or APEST, for short. The apostolic environment creates a setting where other ministries emerge and ministry capacity is maximized.

Practice One: Organize Community around APEST Ministry

Apostolic influence develops ministry capacity largely through calling forth and developing the gifts. It is the foundational gift that provides both the environment and the reference point for the other ministries to flourish as described in Ephesians 4.

Encourage as many people in your community to complete an APEST profile analysis. This will highlight the primary gifts and calling for each person. (For an example of an online APEST profiling tool go to www.theforgottenways.org/apest/.) This is a great resource for communities and leadership teams, as it will allow you to work toward a more complete ministry mix. We also suggest you sign up for the 360-degree evaluation, which allows for a more balanced overview, because it involves others around you in the process. If you choose not to do the 360-degree evaluation, make sure that you talk about it together as a community and give feedback to one another. It's a good idea to graph all the results, so you can see at glance the strengths and weaknesses of your

Mapping the Gifts

Darryn and his mission group have mapped the results of their leadership team on Excel charts[10]. As a team they reflected on the results and hosted a retreat with their whole faith community to reflect how they are positioned as a group. During this time they reviewed their strengths and areas for growth, confirmed one another's gifting, and prayed for one another's development. They also brainstormed how to structure their missionary rhythms in reference to the distribution of the gifts and looked for ways to make room for one another to thrive. Why not try a similar process with your group?

group and areas for growth. This will prove to be a valuable resource in evaluating and planning.

Structuring the community around the fivefold ministry and developing a fully functioning APEST system will go a long way toward maturing an apostolic environment. Endeavor to arrange the community around APEST functions and ensure that all five areas are operational within the leadership group. Custom-build a system that suits your mission group. For instance, this is how South Melbourne Restoration Community reconceived itself around APEST ministries.

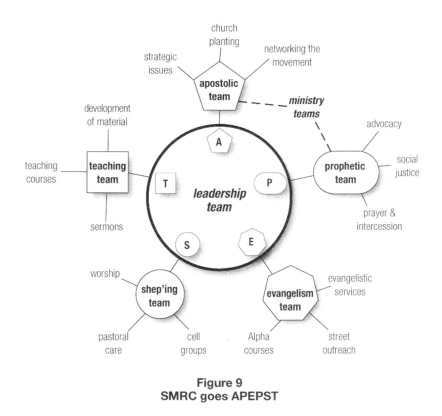

Figure 9
SMRC goes APEPST

Practice Two: Training

To organize a community around APEST, people need to be trained and matured in these functions. This approach allows for a much richer and more biblical typology to inform leadership and ministry development. Furthermore, it allows us to equip the faith community for ministry in every way possible.

Be sure to employ an action-reflection education process based on discipleship processes (see chapter 3). We have discovered through ten years of training missionaries via the Forge Mission Training Network that an action–reflection process is one of the most effective models for missionary development. This process is explained under Habit 2 above (Cultivate Apostolic Genius) and is pretty straightforward—engage in missionary activity, provide a process for reflection and goal setting, and establish theological and missiological frameworks. Here are a few more hints:

- Create an in-house internship process where people are developed in their gifting and calling, where they also learn theory and receive coaching.
- Provide people with resource books, DVDs, articles, and the like.
- Encourage people to attend conferences and workshops.
- Encourage members to participate in other forms of action–reflection training.
- Connect people in context-based networks and learning communities such as Forge (Aus), Shapevine (global), Missio (Forge USA), Ecclesia Network, Epoch Center, Forge Missional Training Network (Canada), Together in Mission (UK), Allelon, DAWN, etc.[11]
- Some members should look into formal seminary training, but we suggest that they take their time and share their insights with, and be held accountable to, their community.

Practice Three: Empower

Empowerment is not something leaders magically give to others. People already have the power. It's not a matter of granting it to them, but of cultivating an environment where they are free to exercise it. We must abandon command-and-control leadership and seek to provide a meaningful context in which people are inspired to exercise their God-given gifts and abilities. As Dee Hock suggests, "If you provide a framework of purpose and principle, people will know what to do in accordance with them, and they'll do it in thousands of unimaginable and creative ways."[12] Apostolic leaders know that missionary coding runs deep within God's people and thus seek to unleash that potential through fashioning a culture where people are empowered into mission-focused ministry.

- Locate innate passions: What are people passionate about? Where does their energy lie? Clever mission groups will build mission around these passions and existing energy.
- Free up time: Don't overprogram and expect people to commit to everything. Limit people's involvement in self-focused in-house activity.
- Seek to integrate life and mission: You have to eat, so why not eat with others? You need to exercise—invite others along. You have to shop for groceries, so make shopping missional. This empowers people to see mission as a way of life rather than as a program.
- Ask probing questions that stir people into action, such as "What was your greatest achievement this past month?" or "What do you wish you had more time for?"
- Defer dreaming to the whole group. Initiate processes for collaborative dreaming.
- Encourage people to experiment with new ideas and approaches.

Habit 5: Catalyze

Apostolic influence seeks to link people, vision, and resources in order to extend Christianity. This is distinctively a catalytic function. Ori Brafman and Rod Beckstrom give the following example of catalytic influence.

> Take nitrogen and hydrogen, two common elements, put them in a container, shut the lid, come back in a day and see the result. Nothing changes. But, if you add iron into the equation, you get ammonia. The interesting thing is that ammonia has no iron in it—it's comprised solely of nitrogen and hydrogen. The iron remains unchanged in the container. It simply facilitates the bonding of these two elements. Iron therefore is a catalyst. It initiates a reaction between elements without fusing into that reaction.[13]

Likewise, catalytic influence in ministry facilitates a meaningful bond between people resulting in positive action. It's an apostolic function in that it inspires people to synergize and work together for a common (kingdom) purpose. Please note that the catalyst function is in no way exclusive to leadership. In fact, there are many people at the grassroots level who operate this way instinctively when they link people together for positive action. The catalyst is the person who always seems to know someone who might help or add value to the task at hand.

As we suggest in the next chapter (on organic systems), this will require leaders to develop a relationally networked system rather than an institutional structure.

Practice One: Initiate Vision and Ideas, Then Step Back

Catalytic people are initiators, idea generators, and inspirers. They are full of new ideas that they allow others to take the responsibility for acting upon. They stay in the background, offering support but providing enough room for people to form and develop ideas in their own way. In many respects the apostles' ministry described in the New Testament was catalytic, as the apostles (Paul in particular) connected people and initiated churches in many new regions.

Here's an example. A catalyst could propose the following question and challenge to the community: "Wouldn't it be great if we could gather a group of young, mission-hearted people to form as a missional band among their friends in the nightclub scene?"

Through this simple question, the vision has been cast, the idea seeded, and the challenge issued. The next step is to wait and see where it finds energy. Occasionally, the catalyst can prod by asking people individually what they thought and how they felt when the idea was shared. In addition to initiating vision and new ideas, the catalyst makes connections among people and provides the essential resources.

Practice Two: Make Connections among People

Catalytic people are not only initiators and idea generators; they are also facilitators and connectors. Brafman and Beckstrom note that if you put a group of people into a room, they might chat about the weather in random groups, but add a catalyst and they'll soon be discussing something specific and purposeful.[14]

Through his or her very presence and example, a catalyst inspires people to connect and talk about things that matter. In a ministry sense, catalysts facilitate discussion and dreaming around participating in God's missionary endeavor. This should happen both formally and informally. Catalysts generally know a lot of people and make connections between individuals with similar direction and passions. They are always thinking, "Who might benefit from knowing whom?" To that end, they intuitively map whom they know, whom those people know, and how they relate to one another and fit into the broader scheme.

- Map connections. Discern the common links, dreams, and passions. Connect the dots between isolated pieces of information.
- Bring people together who have similar passions and callings. Get them sharing their ideas, experiences, and stories.
- Make connections between people's dreams and the necessary resources.
- Read the chapter on the catalyst in *The Starfish and the Spider*, and discuss.
- For more examples on connecting people, please see the networking habit in the next chapter.

Brafman and Beckstrom in their book *The Starfish and the Spider* provide the following table to distinguish the unique difference between a CEO and a catalyst.[15] We find it helpful in thinking about the different ways to influence. For more information, we recommend reading their chapter on the catalyst.

CEO	Catalyst
The boss	A peer
Command and control	Trust
Rational	Emotionally intelligent
Powerful	Inspirational
Directive	Collaborative
In the spotlight	Behind the scenes
Order	Ambiguity
Organizing	Connecting

Group Processing

Session 1: *Explore (talk about it)*

- If you had to highlight one idea from this section, what would it be? Why?

- In your own words, explain apostolic environment to another person in the group. What ideas excite you? Concern you?

- What are the best habits and practices to consider? We have provided a few. Can you think of any others?

- What questions do you have?

- How can you imagine the group growing in this area?

Session 2: *Evaluate (reflect deeper)*

- Is apostolic environment a strength or a weakness for your group?

- Does the majority of the group understand and believe in this concept?

- How is commitment to these ideas already demonstrated in your group? Give examples.

- When was the community best at creating an apostolic environment? What were the contributing factors? What was happening at the time?

- In your opinion, what are the most important issues for creating an apostolic environment?

- What challenges are ahead? What are the barriers? Where do you anticipate resistance?

Session 3: *Employ (act on it)*

- What needs to happen during the next twelve months? What do you need to do that you're not currently doing?

- What will you need to let go of?

- What information and resources will you need? Who else needs to be involved?

- How will you know if you have grown in these areas? What will the key indicators be?

- What habits and practices will you seek to integrate during the next twelve months? List them here.

Action Plans

What are the first steps you will take to achieve these goals? Looking at your past, are they realistic?

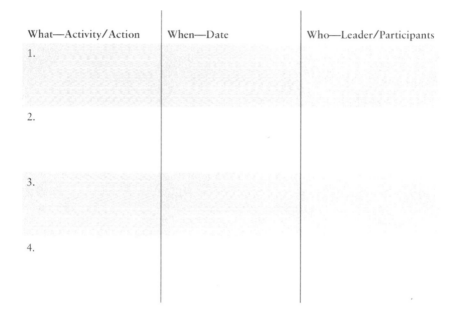

What—Activity/Action	When—Date	Who—Leader/Participants
1.		
2.		
3.		
4.		

Session 4: *Personal Journal*

After processing much information, take some time to pray, listen, and respond to God. How is God prompting you, and how will you respond? Take time to record your impressions as well as insights from the group. Write a prayer expressing your desires to God. If appropriate, share your thoughts in the group, and then pray together.

- What am I sensing from God?

- What is my prayer?

6

Organic Systems

In this chapter we'll explore the next element in mDNA, the inner structures that embody Apostolic Genius and enable organic, exponential, movement-type growth. This chapter will include habits that revolve around developing a movement ethos, structuring as a network, cultivating viruslike growth, and looking at multiplication principles and processes.

The Church as a Living System

Organic descriptions of the church abound in scripture. Images such as body, field, yeast, seeds, trees, and vines are plentiful. These images are not simply metaphors that help us describe a theological truth but actually indicate the way the kingdom operates. When Jesus says "the kingdom of God is like . . . ," he is actually describing the operational principles of kingdom growth. We can therefore look to creation for clues to how God himself intended human life, community, and church to manifest. Having rediscovered the potency of organic systems, we will then need to reappropriate them in the church, in order to reposition us for the challenges and complexities facing us in the twenty-first century.

Followers of Jesus who seek to base their communal life in organic ways find in scripture, as well as in creation, a rich theological resource to fund and sustain it. This is also true for the church. An organic image of church and mission is theologically richer by far than any mechanistic and institutional conceptions of church that we might devise. This is because it is supported by a sense of God's intimate relation and investment in his creation.

An organic, or living systems, approach seeks to structure the common life of an organization around the rhythms and structures that mirror life itself. In this approach we can probe the nature of life and observe how living things organize themselves. From there we can try to emulate as closely as possible this innate capacity of living systems to develop high levels of organization and adapt to varying conditions. Relating a living systems approach to church connects with the idea that every group of God's people has everything within them needed to adapt and thrive in any setting.

A Movement Ethos

But organic systems are not only about the church "greening" its perspectives on organization. They are also about movement dynamics. To recover the missional vitality of the early church, we have to reawaken a movement ethos in our organizations. Most churches have lost any remnant of the type of ethos they had when they started or when their denominations were founded. This is because along the way networks developed into organizations, and organizations developed into institutions. Institutions develop incrementally and are set up to maintain a certain expression by developing rites, rituals, a professional ministry class, buildings, creeds, etc., and to pass them on to succeeding generations. The intentions are usually very sincere, but the net effect often results in a controlling, high-conformity culture that tends to reject efforts to disturb the status quo. Thus, renewal is a difficult process, fraught with the possibility of failure. We do believe that in the end, institutionalization is to some extent inevitable, but we also think it can be held at bay if we are clever about it. Maintaining a movement ethos is one sure antidote to the dangers of increasing institutionalism.

In critiquing religious institutionalism, we are not saying that we don't need some form of structure to maintain healthy spiritual life in the church. We do. But there is a world of difference between organizational *structure* and religious *institution*. We must remember that structure cannot create life, although without it life cannot exist very long. To maintain a movement ethos we need to keep structures as simple as possible and make sure they are easily reproducible.

We can contrast the differences between institutionalized religion and a movement ethos in the following table.

Organic Missional Movement	Institutional Religion
Has pioneering missional leadership as its central role	Avoids leadership based on personality and is often led by an "aristocratic class" who inherit leadership based on loyalty
Seeks to embody the way of life of the Founder	Represents a more codified belief system
Based on internal operational principles (mDNA)	Based increasingly on external legislating policies/governance
Has a cause	Is "the cause"
The mission is to change the future	The mission shifts to preserving the past
Tends to be mobile and dynamic	Tends to be more static and fixed
Decentralized network built on relationships	Centralized organization built on loyalty
Appeals to the common person	Tends to become more and more elitist and therefore exclusive
Inspirational/transformational leadership dominant; spiritual authority tends to be the primary basis of influence	Transactional leadership dominant; institutional authorizing tends to be the primary basis of influence
People of the Way	People of the Book
Centered-set dynamic	Closed-set dynamic

Networked Structures

If Apostolic Genius develops organically and expresses itself in a movement ethos, then it forms itself around a network structure. This is very different from what we have come to expect from our general concept of church.

Peter Ward uses the term "liquid church" to describe what a truly networked church would look like—a church responsive to the increasingly fluid dimension of our culture. He contrasts liquid church with what he calls "solid church." In his terminology, solid church is roughly equivalent to what is here described as "institutional church." And solid church has generally mutated from its original basis as a movement into either (1) communities of heritage (that embody the inherited tradition), (2) communities of refuge (a safe place from the world), or (3) communities of nostalgia (living in past successes).

The alternative is liquid, or networked, church. Networks structure very differently. For one, they are decentralized and are comprised of many different nodes (or agents) in the system. These could be individuals, cells, or organizations. They relate to one another on the basis of relationships and common cause, and not through centralized organization. Therefore, the effective performance of a network over time will depend to a large degree on the cultivation of shared beliefs, principles, interests, and goals. As shocking as it seems at first, it is not hard to see the striking similarities between the structures of terrorist networks like Al-Qaeda and that of the early church. While the agenda for each is entirely different, it is partly the structure that makes both so effective and just about impossible to "take out."

Viruslike Growth

One of the most exciting elements of organic systems is their innate capacity to reproduce, thus allowing for rapid multiplication when conditions are ideal. When applied to the church, rapid multiplication empowers mission and releases movements. The great missiologist Roland Allen called this innate capacity within God's people "the spontaneous expansion of the church." The gospel, like all great ideas, is spread just like a virus. It captures us, and when we are infected, we in turn go on to "infect" others in our relational networks. We can therefore say that in many ways the gospel is "sneezed" and then passed on through further sneezing from one person to another.

Simplicity and Reproducibility

One more thing needs to be noted before we conclude this section, and that is the related issues of reproduction and reproducibility. All organic life seeks to reproduce and perpetuate itself through reproduction, not cloning. This distinction is significant, because many approaches to church planting tend to be more consistent with cloning than reproduction. The result is that of merely duplicating the original model or system from which it came. The trouble is that the problems of the prevailing system are simply imported into the new church without serious reflection.

Reproducibility relates to the capacity of living systems to multiply through simple, reproducible mechanisms. It needs to be embedded in the organic system to ensure that mission will perpetuate. If we are to recover latent Apostolic Genius in the West, then like the Chinese church we must ask ourselves, "What is the irreducible minimum of the faith? What is too complex to reproduce?" We too need to eliminate the things that don't matter. Simplicity is a vital key to multiplication and to spontaneous expansion.

Complex attractional approaches tend to have a contraceptive effect on the reproductive capacities of the church. They can stifle genuine people movements, because effective attractional church requires a professional concept of ministry with a lot of resources. This must sound a clear warning to us as we attempt to negotiate the missional challenges of the twenty-first century. We need to get it right from the start—in the stem cell of the church, so to speak.

When organic systems meet a genuine movement ethos that expresses itself in networked structures, if given the right conditions for reproducibility, then history is in the making. If you'd like to further explore the theory of organic systems, please read chapter 7, as well as the addendum in *The Forgotten Ways*.

Now let us consider specific habits and practices that help form and release organic systems.

Suggested Habits and Practices

Remarkable Jesus movements have the feel of a movement and the structure of an organic network, and they spread like viruses. If we wish to follow in the footsteps of these movements, we must find a pattern of church closer to life itself. In doing this, we suggest the following four habits to awaken and sustain organic growth.

1. Stir up movement
2. Structure organically
3. Network and communicate extensively
4. Sneeze the gospel

Habit 1: Stir Up Movement

It is noteworthy that the Chinese church was truly activated in a powerful way only when all institutional reference points were forcibly removed.[1] To recover the missional vitality of the remarkable Jesus movements, we have to reawaken a movement ethos.

Practice One: Change How You Think about the Church

If we wish to arouse a movement ethos, we must change the way we think about the church. Start to think and talk about the church as a movement rather than as a centralized organization. Seek to awaken the image of Christianity as a movement of disciples whose calling is to "sneeze" the gospel into every imaginable context.

- Educate the group about the nature, flow, and dynamics of movements. A great book to read together is *The Starfish and the Spider*. It's insightful, reasonably short, and very easy to read. Read it together, and then begin to discuss the implications.
- Don't think about church planting, rather think about "movement planting." The reason behind this is to begin with the end in mind.
- Expose the group to stories of dynamic movements. The early church is a great place to start. You will also find numerous examples in *The Starfish and the Spider*, and also in *The Tipping Point*.
- Circulate stories and examples of influential movements, both current and past. Study the Celtic movement, and then translate the applicable principles to your situation.[2]

- Doubt always characterizes decline when it comes to organizational life cycles. You will need to deal with ideological/theological doubt as it arises.

Practice Two: Start to Behave like a Movement

Stirring a movement ethos will require a change in behavior. We not only have to start thinking about the church as a movement, but also need to start behaving like one. Movements are fluid, adaptive, and open to risks, and almost always begin in the grass roots of society. Maybe that's a good place to start.

- Gradually seek to transform the vision from an organization to a movement focus. If you name yourselves as a movement, you will begin to act like one, so start there.
- Consciously begin to structure organically (see habit 2 in this chapter).

Christian Associates International

CAI is a grassroots movement in Europe.[3] In 1999 they set a long-range goal to identify and develop 500 missionaries sent out to establish one or more missional churches in fifty major cities in Europe by 2010—and they are well on the way to achieving this. By explicitly adopting a movement ethos, CAI sees its core task as initiating a chain reaction of church-planting movements. As they see it, a church-planting movement is characterized by habitual church planting. To instill this ethos they've adopted the following four processes:

- Initiating: the process of starting a new church community
- Establishing: the process of community development
- Maturing: the process of growing depth in community
- Reproducing: the church planting process within a church community.

What is absolutely critical to their thinking is the central importance of generating a grassroots movement. This they see as critical for the re-evangelization of post-Christian Europe.[4]

- Create a culture of permission to dream and try new things. Experiment with new mission groups.
- Make it a covenantal requirement for every church or group within your mission to multiply regularly.
- Explore numerous change management processes. You might find one that suits your group perfectly, or you may have to pick and choose from a number of them. A good example of change management process is outlined by Alan Roxburgh and Fred Romanuk in their book *The Missional Leader.*[5]

Habit 2: Structure Organically

All living systems require structure and organization to maintain their existence. An organic approach seeks to structure the common life of a group around the rhythms of life itself. At the heart of organic structure, we find a network of meaningful relationships that unites the whole system. Structure exists to support life, not to obstruct it. So when it starts to inhibit growth, it should be reviewed and modified. The structures need to be simple, reproducible, and internal. When approaching organic structure, think farmer, not CEO; think gardener, not technician.

Practice One: Distribute Power and Function

The role of leadership and the structure it sets in place is to distribute power and function outward in the system (as opposed to centralizing it.) It must cultivate equity, self-sufficiency, and individual opportunity. An organic system recognizes that every member has intelligence and know-how and aims to identify, foster, and unleash that resource. In living systems theory, this is called distributed intelligence; it is spread throughout the organization and can be found at every level. It's essential that each person in the network is empowered to perform according to their gifting and interests. Think of Paul's teachings on the body of Christ in this regard.

In commenting on organic structure, Dee Hock of VISA Corporation advises that the governing structure must not be a chain of command, but a framework for dialogue, deliberation, and coordination among

An Example of Distributing Power

For six years the founding group from TPC met as a leadership team twice per month to review and plan. While these meetings were open to others for their information and input, most regarded this group as the central guiding and decision-making body. The result is that it actually disempowered people to take ownership and participate. After a thorough review of their processes, TPC reworked their structures into a more organic form. Leadership is no longer positional but relational—influence is exercised through relationship and spiritual authority, rather than through an official position. Everyone is involved in brainstorming and planning, and decisions are made by the key stakeholders. They have replaced the team meetings with monthly collaboration and dreaming gatherings.

equals. He suggests power and function must be dispersed to the maximum degree, that participation must be open to all connected parties, and that decisions should be made by groups and methods representing all parties, yet dominated by none.[6]

- Rather than leaders setting direction and making decisions, seek a more community-wide process where all contribute to the issue at hand.
- Try to involve all stakeholders in making decisions. Stakeholders must wear their decisions. If someone is in a decision-making level and doesn't have to live with the consequences of the decision, he or she is not a true stakeholder. Stakeholders are generally those people who have a vested interest in the ministry and have demonstrated that through their actions, devotion, and resources.
- To distribute function, organize the community around individual passions and gifts. For more detail on this, see chapter 4.
- Distribute intelligence by making room in your meetings and other forums for people to share their ideas and findings.
- Encourage ownership and responsibility. This happens largely through involvement in the ministry, as well as through being a part of the dreaming and decision-making processes. For more

information, see the collaboration practice under Networking, below (habit 3).

- Organize regular times when people can contribute to the dreaming and planning.

Practice Two: Become a Learning Organization

A learning organization is one in which people at all levels, individually and collectively, are continually *increasing their capacity* to produce results.[7] It's an organization with an inbuilt philosophy for expecting and responding to change, complexity, and uncertainty. To remain adaptive, we must constantly push the boundaries of our own understanding and knowledge. And we must share and interpret this information throughout the community.

- Encourage those in your community who are avid readers and researchers to share their findings and expand the community with their knowledge.
- Supply accurate and meaningful information, and focus the community around it.
- Empower the apostles, prophets, evangelists, pastors, and teachers to instruct the whole group about their specific area of ministry. You could make it the focus of a five-month community-wide theme— one month to explore the theory and practice of each area.
- Sell the problem before the solution. Always put the problem to the people as the first step, then sit down together and brainstorm a way forward.
- Find a sister community with whom you can covenant to share knowledge and findings.
- Become part of a broader network (see networking habit below).
- Readjust or disband teams as needed.
- Distribute DVDs, books, articles, new research, and other helpful material.
- Attempt to bring meaning, interpretation, and wholeness—rather than order—to chaos.
- Remember that an action–reflection approach is critical to learning.

Practice Three: Structure around Life and Existing Energy

Instead of trying to fit new people, in all their diversity, into a rigid framework, seek to build structure around people's passions, energy, and lifestyles. Aim to build church and mission around people in their context, not the other way around. This means structuring the life of the organization around the life of the people, around the natural ebb and flow of life.

- Build community and mission around existing energy and lifestyles. If there's a group in your church who love to surf, then structure church and mission around them at the beaches and other connected social hubs.
- Find what people are into, what gives them energy, what they spend their time doing, and explore opportunities to frame church and mission around them.
- Choose your gathering (church service) times and frequency carefully. Do they inhibit or promote connection with the broader community you are hoping to reach? Is the time when your church gathers the same time when the host community gathers socially?
- When you notice new energy in your group, poke it, see what makes it tick, and explore ways to support it. Many leaders are intimidated by this, especially if the new energy didn't start with them. Leaders, it's not about you—so get over it and sponsor new grassroots energy and initiatives.
- Be brave and disband groups and ministries that no longer have life in them. If just a few key people constantly have to prop it up, then maybe it's time to put it to bed. Do regular assessments of all groups in the church on this basis.

Practice Four: Shared Belief and Purpose

Networks are held together in a web of meaningful relationships formed around shared belief and purpose. The effective performance of a network will depend on the cultivation of relationships around these two elements. As Dee Hock says:

All organizations are merely conceptual embodiments of a very old, very basic idea—the idea of community. They can be no more or less than the sum of the beliefs of the people drawn to them; of their character, judgments, acts, and efforts. An organization's success has enormously more to do with clarity of a shared purpose, common principles and strength of belief in them than to assets, expertise, operating ability, or management competence, important as they may be.[8]

A community shaped by a sense of common belief and purpose is better than any number of assets or skills. The key is to nurture comradeship around a united belief and sense of purpose in Jesus. This becomes the foundation on which to structure everything else.

- Spend significant time forming a set of common values, beliefs, practices, etc., as already suggested in various elements of mDNA.
- Help new people become familiar with the values, beliefs, and particular calling of the group.
- Host weekend retreats where the story of how and why the ministry began is shared. Use a variety of means to do this: dialogue, story, photos, video, and so on. You can use this environment as a springboard to dream and imagine the future together.
- Aim to distill your identity, purpose, and way of life down to the simplest language possible. It has to be clear and memorable for

Exercise in Evaluating Structures and Processes

1. One at a time, evaluate all your structures and processes.
2. What are their strengths and weaknesses?
3. On a scale of 1–10, do they support or inhibit community, ministry, and mission? (1 = strongly inhibit, 10 = strongly support. Be ruthless with anything below 5.)
4. What structures can be reworked? How would you do it?
5. What structures need to replaced? What are some suggestions for new structures? Do you need to wipe the slate clean and start again? (This could be a viable option; if so, don't be afraid to do it. If you choose this path, make sure you move at a pace set by the community, and be sure to collaborate at all levels.)

TPC: An Example of Structuring Organically

Third Place Communities structures their community in the following way:

Households: These comprise the basic gathering of church. Households meet anywhere—homes, parks, cafés, and they can meet any time. The smaller unit of community gives space for genuine friendships and discipleship to take place. All households meet three times per month and in their own unique way express the values and purposes of TPC. Households are usually no bigger than twenty people.

Tribe: The Tribe is the collection of all TPC households and gathers formally once per month. The Tribe also connects and engages informally through shared projects, proximity in third places, and general life rhythms.

As you can see in the diagram below, the sun symbolizes the core mission and DNA—their identity and ethos. This is what binds them together and is found in every group. The circles represent the principal unit of church (the households), while the arrows signify the multichannel relational networking among the churches. (TPC is also connected to a broader network of missional communities from around the country, which are not pictured in the diagram. This takes place through events, personal visits, e-mail, and phone. This is understood to be the Clan—the family of Tribes.) The Household, the Tribe, and the Clan; they are simple to run and easy to reproduce—most people can do it.

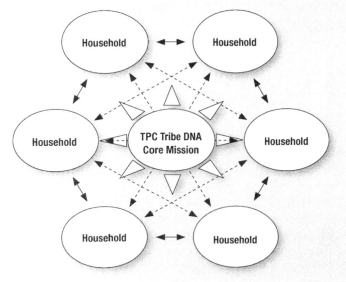

it to be meaningful and embodied. An effective way to do this is through identifying your unique calling and establishing a set of simple missional practices to suit.

- TPC initially developed a set of twelve practices to guide them in living out their calling. They were reasonably straightforward, but there were too many, and they were far too detailed. They weren't easy to remember and definitely were not conversational. A few years later TPC reworked them into a simple list of three practices phrased as one question,[9] to make it easy to remember and talk about. In hindsight this made all the difference for people beginning to live them.

- Honor and encourage one another regularly. Host a meal where you focus the conversation on what you appreciate about the other people in the room. Share what excites you about them, where you see godly traits at work, what they've taught you, the gifts you notice in them, and so on. Use these times to confirm the gifts and value God has invested in them. If you do this often enough, it will become a habit! This will promote shared belief and purpose.

Habit 3: Network and Communicate Extensively

Networking and communication are crucial for organic systems to thrive. A network is a collection of independent people and groups who act autonomously but link across boundaries to work together for a common purpose. The task of leadership is to bring the various elements in the system into meaningful communication and relationship. This will require the leader to focus on developing a relationally networked system rather than an institutional structure for the church.

Practice One: Develop Kingdom Synergy

A key characteristic of missional churches is that they develop meaningful connections beyond the local church. In God's economy the simple but profound reality is that we are much better working together than apart. The problem is that our organizational default tends to focus us on the needs of our own group, and we miss out on the many benefits of networking with others. The beauty about networking is that the outcome is often greater than the sum of the parts. When diverse gifts and knowledge rub up against each other, new forms of knowledge and possibilities arise. This is kingdom synergy.

- Create a large pool of missional practitioners and communities. These colleagues will prove to be valuable allies. Locate them, recognize and honor their good ideas and habits, swap findings, and seek to learn from one another.
- Before making new plans, look around to see if anyone else in the broader network is doing something similar to what you hope to achieve. Don't reinvent the wheel if you can legitimately collaborate with and learn from others.
- Combine your resources and train people together. That might mean cooperating on a series of workshops or intensives or may even equate to an in-depth internship-style program. But remember not to totally outsource the training function, or you will eventually lose the capacity to train locally.
- Host regular network days and workshops.
- Develop a resource bank and make it available across the network.
- Organize a retreat with another missional group. Hanging out together over a weekend sharing food, life, and stories is an effective way to inspire and energize both groups.
- Have communion together often. At the heart of this practice is the recognition that Jesus is in our midst and that we are united and brought together through him.

Practice Two: Ensure Flow of Information

The free flow of information is vital for the health and growth of a network. Leaders of networks don't withhold information to use as *power*; they share it widely and use it to *empower*. That's a big difference.

- Church newsletters and calendars are significant communication tools for sharing new information and updating people on what's

Information Flow at VISA

"The greatest delight from all my days leading Visa, were open staff meetings, from which we never wavered. Within a day after every board meeting, staff meetings were held to include every employee of the company at every level including the newest. They were conducted by the most senior person present. At the meeting, every decision of the board was fully disclosed. Every employee was free to ask any question about the decisions, or anything else of concern to them. Their questions were answered fully. 'That's confidential' was not considered an answer. 'I don't know but I will find out and tell you at the next meeting' was permissible, but only if the promise was faithfully kept."[10] (Dee Hock, Founder of the VISA company)

happening around the traps. Take pride in this communiqué; don't just slap it together in a few minutes. It's a core information-sharing tool for your group.

- When you gather, have significant time set aside for people to share.
- Regularly send out articles through e-mail, and point people to Web sites and other important resources.
- Talk about and promote books for people to read. Maybe review and recommend a book each month. Start a book club where people read the book of the month and then catch up for a chat and coffee.
- Provide details: we must empower people to communicate with each other individually and as a whole group. To do this, people will need each other's contact details. Provide access to a database with such details, including e-mail lists.
- Provide communication tools: if people are going to communicate with one another, they will need the means to do so. Set up an Internet group so people can communicate with one another simply and easily. Social utility Web sites such as Facebook are great for this. It's simple to set up your own group. Anyone can upload information, messages, links to Web sites, resources, photos, and

videos. Members can easily message one another individually or send a message to the whole group without typing addresses. Myspace, Bebo, Orkut, hi5, and many other social networking sites provide similar services, all for free.

- You could also develop a group on shapevine.com and use the video conferencing features. Shapevine is dedicated to the development of decentralized Christian networks and education.

Practice Three: Collaborate and Dream Together

Defer idea generation to the whole church community as much as possible. When you need fresh ideas, or wish to discover a new way forward, or begin to plan for a new mission initiative, include everyone in the process. Don't simply brainstorm as a small team, but extend the task to the crowd. It will foster ownership, and in the end you will receive a higher quality of ideas than if you just did it among yourselves. As a team, don't plan everything, but rather seek to awaken the dream and ideas from others. Smart missional leaders will work out how to tap into this resource and unleash the genius from within.

The function of leadership here is to set the context for collaboration. The next step is to interpret what the group is saying and communicate it back to them in a meaningful framework consistent with the group's calling. Here are a few questions to stir your group's missionary imagination:

- What is God preparing us for? How can we play our part in expanding God's mission?

How Google Creates New Ideas

A great example of this process is found in the way Google generates new ideas. All workers are encouraged to post new ideas on the Google intranet. Periodically, everyone gets the chance to review and vote for their favorite ideas. The top ideas are given time and resources for development and, hopefully, implementation. The person who dreamed up the idea is given time off their regular work to develop their idea with a small team. What a brilliant ethos! Imagine if every church did this in relation to new mission.

More Ideas for Imagining and Collaborating

- Organize regular brainstorming sessions.
- Host weekend retreats for dreaming and collaborating about future plans and new mission initiatives.
- Encourage members to share ideas with one another. Adopt a Google-like process as mentioned above.
- Here is a simple exercise that can be done with your community or leadership team:
  - Draw on three bits of paper three images or phrases that illustrate your dream for mission as you imagine it three years from now.
  - Share those dreams in pairs.
  - Ask each pair to choose two of their six dreams to bring to the larger group and place on a board.
  - Once the dreams are all posted, cluster the dreams into themes, and give one title per cluster.
  - Each person then picks the cluster they resonate with most.
  - Working in small groups, flesh out the dreams and brainstorm into actionable steps.

- How can we multiply our communities?
- What would our host community look like with God at the core?
- Where is God already at work in the community around us? How can we join God in what he's doing?
- What is good news for the people and culture we're connecting with?

Practice Four: Always Seek a Win-Win Outcome

Healthy networks are built on the idea of win-win alliances. The outcomes from this approach are synergistic in that they are mutually beneficial. Win-win is a belief based on the idea that there is often a third alternative. Character, relationship, respect, and appreciation are the foundations of win-win. We have found Stephen Covey's Seven Habits very helpful in training people in this approach, particularly the three social habits.[11]

- Read Covey's *Seven Habits of Highly Effective People*, especially the social habits. Discuss these and consider how they enhance a networking ethos.
- Translate these meaningfully into your church and organizational life.
- Forget self-promotion. Do what you can to help others succeed in mission.
- Avoid the other options: win-lose, lose-win, lose-lose, and win. None of these are helpful alternatives.
- See the issue from another point of view. Seek first to understand, then to be understood.
- Identify the key issues and concerns involved.
- Determine what results would constitute a fully acceptable solution.
- Identify possible new options to achieve those results.

Habit 4: Sneeze the Gospel

One of the most powerful elements of organic systems is the innate capacity to reproduce spontaneously and exponentially. The habit, "sneezing the gospel," in essence is focused on the church's ability to create an environment where the gospel and witnessing community grows naturally and swiftly.

The gospel itself is a very powerful idea that can spread just like a virus if the conditions are right. The rapid and spontaneous growth of the early church is testament to this fact. The setting was just right; there was a common language, a predominant culture, and, thanks to the Romans, extensive infrastructure. Not to mention a widespread spiritual hunger brought about by the meaninglessness of paganism. As people freely traveled around the known world, the gospel was "sneezed" and passed on through further sneezing from one person to another. From twenty-five thousand to twenty million in two hundred years, that's epidemic! We suggest that sneezing the gospel is enhanced when we *aim for simplexity, release early and often*, and *aim for viruslike growth*. These are the three practices we recommend.

Practice One: Aim for Simplexity

The term *simplexity* is taken from the realm of biology, where it brings together two key ideas that are critical to organic systems—namely, simplicity and complexity. What occurs in movements is the capacity to distill a message to its core while at the same time retaining both its original meaning and depth. "Jesus is Lord" is one such example. It captures a complex idea of monotheism in one simple, three-word confession. This is not only sneezable, but also profoundly transformative.

To sneeze the gospel, both the message and message community must be easily and rapidly transferred. The motto here is simple to get, simple to spread. Remember that when Paul goes into Thessalonica, he is kicked out nine days later, and he can write two letters to them and call them a church. In the West, we have complicated and intellectualized the gospel. The problem is that the more complex the message, the slower the possibility of quick adoption. We need to learn again from the phenomenal movements of history. Until we do so, exponential growth will evade us.

- Distill the gospel to its most pure and simple. What are the core essentials, its irreducible minimum? Make sure you connect this with the existential need of people you are trying to reach.
- We need to refine our ideas until they are thoroughly "sneezable" by anyone.
- The same is true for the organizational ethos. Develop simple ways of expressing the ideas that describe as well as mobilize the church. In this way it becomes sneezable.
- Make church as simple and reproducible as possible. Keep each core unit of church small and simple to run, easy to duplicate.
- Avoid clutter, people have enough already: *shed all that does not matter*.

Practice Two: Release Early and Often

This phrase, taken from the software development world, is the idea that underlies the release of beta versions of software. By releasing software before it is fully completed, the programmers receive significant feedback from users and add it to the solution to create a better product. Likewise, we suggest that you encourage innovation and experimentation, but that you don't wait for the perfect plan. People will learn on the way in the place of action.

- Develop a culture of feedback from all stakeholders. Learn from mistakes.
- Regularly research new areas for mission. Get as many people in your groups as possible to be involved in this. Don't just leave it to leadership.
- Continually recruit and prepare new teams as suggested in the chapter on apostolic environment.
- Periodically gather together all the mission bands across your community (or network) for mutual learning, reflection, and encouragement.
- Consistently equip and energize all mission groups. Remember that they are the heroes and ought to feel deeply valued by leadership.
- Build new expressions of church around new believers. Don't absorb them all into one community. Each group should be taught basic missionary skills of contextualizing gospel and community.

The Starfish and the Spider

Spiders are creatures with eight legs coming out of a central body, and if you look closely, you will see a spider also has a head with eight eyes. If you chop off the spider's head, it dies. It could possibly survive without a leg or two but certainly wouldn't survive without its head. At first glance, a starfish looks similar to a spider. Like the spider, the starfish appears to have a bunch of legs coming out of a central body. But that's where the similarities end. The starfish doesn't have a head, and its central body is not in charge. In fact, the major organs are replicated throughout each and every arm. If you cut the starfish in half, it won't die; instead, you'll have two starfish to deal with. Some varieties can replicate from just a single piece of arm. They can achieve this magical regeneration because a starfish is basically a network of cells, with everything it needs to reproduce spread throughout the entire body.[12]

Remember, they are not necessarily running large organizations but rather simple churches.

- Build new mission around people's passions, gifts, and lifestyles.

Practice Three: Aim for Viruslike Growth

In setting up an organic system to enhance the church's reproductive capacity, we are essentially aiming for spontaneous, viruslike growth. The gospel should be simple to get and simple to pass on, just like a virus.

- Watch the movie *Pay It Forward* and discuss the principles involved.
- Be persistent. All ideas that have gone viral were persistent to the point of hitting a critical mass, after which the idea moved to spontaneous growth. But be careful not to bug people to the point of annoyance.
- Think and pray carefully about the initial host community you befriend. Are they open to your group and core values? Do you already have significant connections there? Is this host group well connected and networked? Will they introduce you to others in the community (recall the "person of peace" concept of Luke 10).
- As we have suggested, keep the core components of church simple, reproducible and small. Keeping the core unit of church small increases your surface area, providing increased proximity and offering the host community numerous connection points.
- Imagine if everyone in your community took a multiplication approach to mission. Consider the following exercise:

Assume you have twenty-five members.
  * Each person covenants to bring five people to Jesus in a ten-year period. Include a commitment to disciple and challenge them to do the same (five people each).

The Tipping Point

Malcolm Gladwell, in his book *The Tipping Point*, highlights the mechanisms by which some ideas achieve popularity while others fade into oblivion. He unveils a number of similar patterns at play in nearly every influential trend. Gladwell identifies three key factors that determine whether a trend will *tip* into wide-scale popularity.[13] While we know that the gospel is far more than an idea, these findings highlight the elements that amplify the flow of ideas. We found this helpful as a template for reflecting on our own local ministry; we hope you do as well.

1. The Law of the Few
   Success is largely dependent on the involvement of people with a distinct and rare set of social skills. To attain widespread popularity, a few key people must champion an idea before it can reach the tipping point. They are known as connectors, mavens, and salesmen. The aim is to identify and use these people types in getting an idea off the ground.

   Connectors are people who link us with other people. They are individuals who know lots of people and have ties in many different social contexts. Connectors act as conduits between people, helping create connections and relationships. You know these people. They are those with apostolic, hospitality, evangelistic, pastoral, and serving traits.
   Mavens are those we rely upon to connect us with new information. They accumulate knowledge, know how to share it with others, and have a strong compulsion to help people make informed decisions. You know these folk as well. They are people with gifts of wisdom, knowledge, prophecy, faith, discernment, and teaching,
   Salesmen are persuaders, who have a noticeable quality that goes beyond what they say, influencing others to want to agree and join with them. These are predominantly the evangelists, prophets, teachers, and apostles in your midst.
2. The Stickiness Factor
   This refers to the unique quality that compels an idea to "stick" and influence new behavior. It is often counterintuitive to popular wisdom and inspires people to pay close attention. Stickiness is hard to define, and its presence or absence often relies heavily on context. What helps the gospel stick? Incarnating the gospel in life and community, credibility, personal testimony, acts of generosity and kindness, hospitality, extravagant love for the world and its inhabitants, to mention a few.

Six Principles for stickiness:[14]

1. Simplicity. "To strip an idea down to its core, we must be masters of exclusion. We must relentlessly prioritize. Saying something short is not the mission—sound bites are not the ideal. Proverbs are the ideal. We must create ideas that are both simple and profound" (16).

2. Unexpectedness. "We need to violate people's expectations. We need to be counterintuitive." "We can use surprise—an emotion whose function is to increase alertness and cause focus—to grab people's attention." "For our idea to endure, we must generate interest and curiosity" (116).

3. Concreteness. "We must explain our ideas in terms of human actions, in terms of sensory information." "In proverbs, abstract truths are often encoded in concrete language: 'A bird in hand is worth two in the bush'" (17).

4. Credibility. "Sticky ideas have to carry their own credentials. We need ways to help people test our ideas for themselves. . . ." Ronald Reagan asked, "Before you vote, ask yourself if you are better off today than you were four years ago" (17).

5. Emotions. "How do we get people to care about our ideas? We make them feel something." "We are wired to feel things for people, not for abstractions. Sometimes the hard part is finding the right emotion to harness" (17–18).

6. Stories. "How do we get people to act on our ideas? We tell stories." "Hearing stories acts as a kind of mental flight simulator, preparing us to respond more quickly and effectively" (18).

3. The Power of Context

If the environment or historical moment in which an idea is introduced is not right, it's not as likely to spread. While a variety of complex factors and variables play a role in sparking a trend, it's often a few small but influential changes in an environment that allow these factors to tip. Think John 4, and the Samaritan Woman at the well. That very interaction with one person tipped the town of Sychar into belief. In fact, Jesus pointed to the power of context and timing when he said, in verse 35, ". . . open your eyes and look at the fields! They are ripe for harvest."

When conditions are right, receptivity to the idea will be high. If receptivity is not high, then work on the conditions, not the idea.

* Let's say this cycle was repeated five times in ten years, just once every two years. The outcome would be 78,215 new disciples. Not bad for twenty-five people!
* Now imagine that every church covenanted to do the same, to plant five churches every ten years. And then those churches took the challenge and started another five . . . and so the cycle goes.

Group Processing

Session 1: *Explore (talk about it)*

- If you had to highlight one idea from this section, what would it be? Why?

- In your own words, explain organic systems to another person in the group. What ideas excite you? Concern you?

- What are the best habits and practices to consider? We have provided a few. Can you think of any others?

- What questions do you have?

- How can you imagine the group growing in this area?

Session 2: *Evaluate (reflect deeper)*

- Are organic systems a strength or a weakness for your group?

- Does the majority of the group understand and believe in this concept?

- How is commitment to these ideas already demonstrated in your group? Give examples.

- When was the community best at creating organic systems? What were the contributing factors? What was happening at the time?

- In your opinion, what are the most important issues for implementing an organic system?

- What challenges are ahead? What are the barriers? Where do you anticipate resistance?

Session 3: *Employ (act on it)*

- What needs to happen during the next twelve months? What do you need to do that you're not currently doing?

- What will you need to let go of?

- What information and resources will you need? Who else needs to be involved?

- How will you know if you have grown in these areas? What will the key indicators be?

- What habits and practices will you seek to integrate during the next twelve months? List them here.

Action Plans

What are the first steps you will take to achieve these goals? Looking at your past, are they realistic?

What—Activity/Action	When—Date	Who—Leader/Participants
1.		
2.		
3.		
4.		

Session 4: *Personal Journal*

After processing much information, take some time to pray, listen, and respond to God. How is God prompting you, and how will you respond? Take time to record your impressions as well as insights from the group. Write a prayer expressing your desires to God. If appropriate, share your thoughts in the group, and then pray together.

- What am I sensing from God?

- What is my prayer?

7

Communitas,
Not Community

In December 2004 something both dreadful and remarkable happened—the Asian tsunami that killed about 250,000 people provoked what was undoubtedly one of the most amazing explosions of worldwide generosity and compassion in recent history. In and through the sheer horror of the tsunami, people found one another in a new and remarkable way. This is an example of *communitas*, and it is exactly this aspect of humanity that will be explored in this chapter. *Communitas* takes many forms, but whatever the form, it describes the type of comradeship that was and is experienced in the phenomenal Jesus movements, and so is an essential element of Apostolic Genius. Both the Early Christian movement and the church in China experienced one another in the context of a shared ordeal that bound them together in a much deeper form of community than we have become accustomed to. For our purposes here, we can define *communitas* as the type of community that develops in the context of danger, an ordeal, or an overwhelming task. It happens when, faced with such a challenge, the participants "find each other" in a new and deeper way. The social bonds are strengthened and restructured. Friends become comrades.

Liminality and *Communitas*

To come to grips with the dynamics of movements that change the world, we have found Victor Turner's ideas of *liminality* and *communitas* particularly useful.[1] Turner was an anthropologist who studied various rites of passage among African people groups and came up with the term *liminality* to describe the transition process accompanying a fundamental change of state or social position. Situations of liminality in this context can be extreme, where the participant is cast out of the normal structures of life, is humbled, disoriented, and subjected to various rites of passage, which together constitute a test of whether the participant will be allowed back into society and to transition to the next level in the prevailing social structure. Liminality therefore applies to that situation where people find themselves in an in-between, marginal state in relation to the surrounding society, a place that could involve significant danger and disorientation, but not necessarily so.

For example, in many tribes all across Africa, younger boys are kept under the care of the women until initiation age—around thirteen. At the appropriate time, the men sneak into the female compound of the village at night and "kidnap" the lads. The boys are blindfolded, roughed up, and herded out of the village and taken into the bush. They are then circumcised and left to fend for themselves in the wild for a period lasting up to six months. Once a month, the elders of the tribe go to meet them to help debrief and mentor them. But at first they have to find both inner and outer resources to cope with the ordeal pretty much by themselves. During this time, the initiates move from being disoriented and individualistic to developing a bond of comradeship forged in the testing conditions of liminality. This sense of comradeship and communality that comes out of the shared ordeal Turner calls *communitas*. *Communitas* in his view *happens* in situations where individuals are driven to find one another through a common experience of ordeal, humbling, transition, and marginalization. It involves intense feelings of social togetherness and belonging brought about by having to rely on one another in order to survive. If the boys emerge from these experiences, they are reintroduced to the tribe as men. They are thus accorded the full status of manhood—they are no longer considered boys.

So the related ideas of liminality and *communitas* describe the dynamics of the Christian community inspired to overcome their instincts to "huddle and cuddle" and instead form themselves around a common mission that calls them to a dangerous journey. *Communitas* is always linked with the experience of liminality. It involves adventure and movement and describes that unique experience of togetherness that only really happens among a group of people inspired by the vision of a better world who attempt to do something about it.

Significant manifestations of Apostolic Genius teach us that liminality and *communitas* are the *normative situation* of the pilgrim people of God. This is certainly the case for the phenomenal Jesus movements in view. It is in their shared ordeal that these movements thrive. In this perspective, the phenomenal Jesus movements were/are expressions of *communitas*, and not community as we normally conceive it.

The Bible and *Communitas*

The claim that *communitas* and liminality are normative for God's people is thoroughly biblical. Take Abram, for instance, who with his entire extended family is called by God to leave house and home to undertake a very risky journey to an unknown land. And when we look at the experiences they have along the way, the stories that have shaped all subsequent faith, we see that they are not safe little bedtime stories. Rather they call us to a dangerous form of faithfulness that echoes the faithfulness of Abraham (Gal. 3:15ff.; Heb. 11:9–13). Or when we explore the profoundly liminal exodus experience, we find that this very tricky journey permanently shaped the people of God and continues to do so to this day. The same can be said of the exile into Babylon centuries later. When we consider the lives and ministries of Samuel, Elijah, Samson, and David and his band, and we ask what conditions they encountered, we come up with the consistent themes of liminality and *communitas*.

When we come to the New Testament, we need only to look to the life of Jesus. He had nowhere to lay his head, and he discipled his followers *on the road* in the dangerous conditions of an occupied land, against a hostile religious elite. Look at the life of Paul. He describes it vividly in 2 Corinthians. The book of Acts is so filled with *communitas* and liminality that it reads like a rollicking adventure story. It seems that liminality and *communitas* are normative for the people of God in the Bible and in the Jesus movements of history. How did we ever lose this perspective?

It's Everywhere!

It's hard not to spot this type of communal experience in so many aspects of our lives. Already mentioned are those times of disaster, but *communitas* can be found in far more common situations like athletic teams, adventure camps, and short-term missions. *Communitas* also features in just about every movie, but particularly in adventure movies of various sorts. Consider the mythic truth in *The Lord of the Rings*. This great story highlights the fact that the "Fellowship of the Ring" actually becomes a *real* fellowship only as it undergoes great struggle and hardship in the face of overwhelming evil. By undertaking this seemingly impossible task, and by facing hardships together, the group actually becomes a *communitas*. They discover one another in a way they could not in any other circumstance. Here is the mythic representation of *mission*—nothing less than the destruction of evil in the world; *discipleship*—constantly choosing goodness in the face of overwhelming opposition; and *communitas*—becoming a great community together in pursuit of a mission. These stories have power over us because they awaken something deep inside us—the abiding human need for adventure, journey, and comradeship.

Artificial Environments and the Death of *Communitas*

The loss of *communitas* also has massive implications for churches and other types of organizations. Without any real engagement with the "outside world," churches quickly become sheltered, artificial environments that are safeguarded from the danger and disturbances in the surrounding environment. They become missionally unresponsive. They become closed systems with their own peculiar cultures that have little relational, social, and cultural associations to the world outside. The problem is that when a system is closed and artificial, and has generally not cultivated adaptability and internal variety, it will ultimately deteriorate toward equilibrium. And in living systems, total equilibrium means death. Contrary to what we might feel, danger and risk can be good, even necessary, for us.

The Future and the Shaping of Things to Come

Cultivating a vigorous transformative vision can also create liminality and *communitas*. Holding a definite sense of vision and mission informs and alters how people think and behave in the present. When we are caught up in a vision and pursue it, we are changed, and we go on to enact history. This is exactly what is meant by the phrase "managing from the future." This way of approaching organizational development means establishing a compelling goal that draws the organization out of its comfort zone. This concept of planning from the future is a key activator of mission and therefore a direct function of missional leadership. In many ways, this is how the kingdom of God works. It is God's future pressing itself in on us. It not only creates liminality, but should result in *communitas*.

Mission as Organizing Principle

Another liminal factor is to organize the church's life around mission (our role outside of the church), not ministry (our relationships with one another). Pastor Gordon Cosby[2] noted that in over sixty years of ministry, he had observed that no groups that came together around a nonmissional purpose ever ended up becoming missional. It was only those groups that set out to be missional that actually got around to doing it. If evangelizing and discipling the nations lies at the heart of the church's purpose in the world, then it is mission, and not ministry, that is the true organizing principle of the church. By planting the flag outside the walls and boundaries of the church, so to speak, the church discovers itself by rallying to it. If the church organizes around mission, then ministry naturally follows, because ministry is the *means* by which we accomplish mission.

As observed earlier, in chapter 2, dualism is the belief that the world is separated into spiritual and nonspiritual realms. The issue of dualism is raised again here because, although Christians largely reject this philosophy, we still tend to embody this belief in our structures and activities. In a diagram that reworks a previous version, we can illustrate what this might look like.

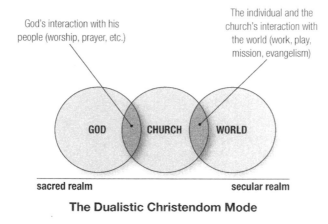

God's interaction with his people (worship, prayer, etc.)

The individual and the church's interaction with the world (work, play, mission, evangelism)

GOD   CHURCH   WORLD

sacred realm   secular realm

The Dualistic Christendom Mode

There is another way to configure these three elements that is much more integrated and biblical. This will simply involve reconfiguring the relation of God, world, and church. When we can conceive the three circles intersecting at the center, there we have a church that is truly missional, is deeply incarnational, and is acting in a way that extends the ministry of Jesus into the world. The fact is that God is everywhere. He is already deeply involved in all people's lives. The church needs to adjust its position in relation to God and the world, and in doing so we must break the bondage of dualism.

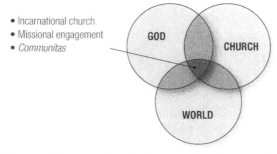

• Incarnational church
• Missional engagement
• *Communitas*

GOD   CHURCH

WORLD

Missional-Incarnational *Communitas* Approach

One of the things that the story of Abraham, the fellowship of sports teams, and the story of the *Lord of the Rings* teach us is that the journey itself is important. They show that a deep form of togetherness and love is found when we embark on a common mission of discovery and danger and have to find one another in the process. We need to hit the road again. We are the people of the Way, and our path lies before us. In trying to rearticulate the nature of authentic Christian community, that of a *communitas* formed around a mission and undertaken by a group of uncertain but brave comrades, by evoking mythic imagery from great stories and calling to mind how Jesus and the early church spread the message, we evoke that yearning to undertake an adventurous journey of rediscovery of that ancient force called Apostolic Genius.

Suggested Habits and Practices

Communitas is an essential element of Apostolic Genius, as it describes the kind of deep comradeship that is experienced in phenomenal Jesus movements. If we wish to fashion the same level of togetherness and solidarity, we will need to embark on a mission that follows Jesus beyond our comfort zone into every nook and cranny of society. There, and only there, will we encounter true *communitas*. As a way to "hit the road" again, we suggest exploring the following four habits and related practices.

1. Develop a transformative vision
2. Position the church within the hub of life
3. Engage in shared endeavors
4. Put adventure back into the venture

Habit 1: Develop a Transformative Vision

The first habit we suggest in fostering *communitas* is to develop a transformative vision. Calling people to a clear and compelling future can influence how they behave in the present and lead the group into genuine expressions of *communitas*. Developing a transformative goal that draws the organization out of its comfort zone is a key habit in creating camaraderie. Here are a few suggestions in beginning to do that.

Practice One: Create a Daring Vision

A great way to foster camaraderie is to gather the community around a collective vision that propels them out of their context and into their preferred future. The important word here is *collective*—for people to own it, they must be part of shaping it and be captivated by it. It must gather the dreams of individuals and integrate them meaningfully into a common dream.

- Dream and collaborate. It's important to do this as a community. We have already explored this in some depth in the section on organic systems, so if you'd like more suggestions, we refer you to that section.
- Once the daring vision is developed, talk about it a lot, and together find simple ways to begin to act it out.
- Manage from the future. Establish a broad missional vision and rally the community around it. This is what is meant by managing from the future—define the goal and move toward it.

Practice Two: Learn about Communitas Together

Secondly, the process of exploring images and ideas relating to *communitas* is another key building block in fostering a compelling vision and common purpose. The key word is *together*. The process is just as valuable as the information, as it will nurture a sense of cohesion and shared purpose.

- Provide biblical examples of *communitas*. You will find them throughout the scriptures, from Genesis to Revelation.
- Watch movies together, and then reflect. These stories have influence because they awaken our need for adventure, journey, and comradeship. For suggested movies, see the resource section.

- As a community, work your way through books and articles that relate to *communitas*. Read, dream, and discuss. A good place to start is to read chapter 5 in *Exiles* by Michael Frost.[3]
- Give people a taste of *communitas*. There's nothing like being able to point to personal experience. In reflecting on people's experience, uncover the importance and necessity of *communitas* in advancing the mission of Jesus. This will move theory into reality.
- Organize a short-term mission trip. This could be overseas or local. In reflecting on the group's experience of *communitas*, ask how this can become the normative experience for God's people.

Habit 2: Position the Church within the Hub of Life

Our tendency as the people of God is to separate ourselves from the world and create sacred places to fellowship, worship, and engage with God. As we have seen, this sacred/secular dualism has plagued the church, and while we reject this philosophy, we still tend to practice it in our structures, activity, and positioning. The outcome is that we create artificial environments that lead us away from real life and far from *communitas*. A nondualistic approach seeks interplay among God, the world, and the church. In the terminology of this book, this will mean to become missional-incarnational, which in turn will engender authentic *communitas*.

Practice One: Build Church around People, Not People around Church

By positioning the church in the hub of life, we mean building church and all its components in the context of life, as opposed to removed from it. Now, we don't mean running a church service in a pub on a Sunday morning when none of the regular patrons are present. We're referring to something a lot more integrated and contextual than that. And this applies not just to the church service, but to the entire life of the church—its fellowship, learning, worship, evangelism, care for the poor, pursuit of justice, stewardship, and so on. Building church around people seriously considers the host community when arranging each and every aspect of its life—its structure, activity, and positioning.

- Avoid artificial religious environments. They are detrimental to a vigorous spiritual life.
- Think creatively and brainstorm how you can rearrange your church in the context of the broader community in which you are located.
- Evaluate your structures and activities. Do they inhibit or promote connection with the broader community? Do they remove the church from real life or locate the group within the hub of life? Are your gatherings accessible and understandable?
- Identify your worship elements, and ask where else in society they occur. This will help in seeking a nondualistic experience that directly relates to your host community.

Green Spaces

In San Francisco a group called ReImagine refers to different colored spaces. Yellow space refers to a Christian spirituality that is concerned only with the personal, interior world of faith. It characterizes the classic individualized form of faith that focuses on personal quiet times, Bible study, church attendance, and personal ethical behavior. Blue space refers to an exclusively other-focused form of Christian spirituality, one that takes context seriously and features such activities as social concern, justice seeking, activism, and public ethical behavior. It is only in the interaction between them that we come close to biblical missional activity and spirituality, as shown in the diagram below. Since the combination of yellow and blue on the color chart does make green, it's a clever way to think about missional spaces. In a Green Space, story and context, the individual and the communal, the interior world and the exterior world, the religious and the nonreligious, find genuine meeting.[4]

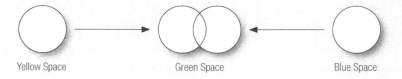

Yellow Space   Green Space   Blue Space

Practice Two: Keep the Missional-Incarnational Approach in Mind

While we have explored this theme at length in its own chapter, it's important to highlight this movement as central in creating genuine *communitas* through locating the church in the midst of life. To experience the kind of solidarity common to the early church, today's church will need to activate this impulse as its primary posture.

- Reread chapter 4 to become familiar with the ideas and examples.
- As a group, create your own ideas that are best suited to your group and context.
- Seek to integrate proximity, frequency, and spontaneity into the life of the church.

Habit 3: Engage in Shared Endeavors

The next habit we suggest in experiencing *communitas* is to get involved in shared endeavors with those in your immediate community. By this we mean taking part in projects that situate you shoulder-to-shoulder in meaningful endeavor with others in your church *as well as* with people in the broader, non-Christian community. This includes working side-by-side with the host community on meaningful initiatives, but it also involves engaging together in mission with other Christians. Yes, this means that you *can* experience *communitas* with people in the church as well as with those beyond the church. Obviously, the experience will be different in each case, but both are highly important and missional. The unique experience of *communitas* occurs when a group of people inspired by the vision of a better world actually attempts to do something about it together.

Practice One: Joint Community Projects

Joint community projects are about engaging as a faith community in initiatives shoulder-to-shoulder with members from the local (host) community. Earlier in this book,[5] we briefly looked at the idea of

Murals in San Francisco

Mark Scandrette is an amazing urban missionary in bohemian San Francisco. One of the projects he's helped initiate is a mural art co-op that gathers to paint walls throughout the city. The co-op secures the project, then gathers to decide what they want to communicate through the mural. After much discussion about politics, religion, meaning, and the like, they decide on a theme. They divvy up the mural, so each member receives a section. It's their task to design that part of the mural to make it fit in with the general theme and the work of the other members. Having done the conceptual design, they gather every Saturday, armed with stepladders and materials, and spend the whole day painting and chatting, as well as sharing lunch and maybe a few beers at the end of the day. The project can take up to three months to complete, and by the end of it, they have delved deep into each other's lives and explored many themes related to life, God, and spirituality. Most of all, they have become good friends.[6]

shared projects as a way to build meaningful connection with those beyond the church. Joint community projects are the same—they are highly missional and a great way to build *communitas*. In working together on community-wide projects, significant connection and camaraderie naturally develop. Here are a few of our suggestions; however, it's best that you create your own ideas related to your context.

- Care for the environment together. There are bound to be numerous projects in your area to get involved with. If not, then create one, but do it in conjunction with members of the local community.
- Organize or support community fundraisers or awareness raisers for local nonprofit groups.
- Volunteer a day a month for a local nonprofit group.
- Pursue justice together. There are always local and global issues in need of volunteers and support.
- Organize an overseas trip to a developing nation to serve others in need. Be mindful that the project is not too religious, where members are asked to run Sunday school for the local children.

A Local Business
Takes Initiative

A friend who owns and operates a small physiotherapy business has adopted an overseas development project that as a company they support financially. What's impressive is that they not only support the venture with their money, but also give their staff time off from regular duties to travel overseas to visit and serve this project. Imagine if all Christian business owners did that with their non-Christian staff! What a great way to build meaningful engagement and *communitas* with employees and coworkers.

Make it far more practical, so those beyond the church will feel like they can contribute meaningfully.

Practice Two: Engage in Mission Together

While joint community projects locate you side-by-side members of the host community, this practice is specifically about *engaging in mission and evangelism together with other Christians*. Through the experience of shared mission, a faith community will instill a "me for the community and the community for the world" ethos. As a result, camaraderie will form around a common sense of missional purpose. It's helpful to encourage rhythms in which people can engage in mission together on a regular basis. Here are a few examples:

- Join a local sporting group together with a few members from your church.
- Organize a book club, go for a regular bike ride with others, or hang out weekly at the same social venue.
- Since 2002, Third Place Communities have practiced the regular rhythm of going to the same pub every Sunday afternoon. This has been a great opportunity for engaging the broader community with the gospel.
- Every Tuesday night, a friend of ours goes out with a guy from his church. Together, they invite a mutual friend or someone from work who is not a Christian. This has become a practice for them.

- Another group of Christians we know get together every week to share a meal and watch a popular TV series with some of their friends from work.

Whatever you choose, remember that the point is to engage in mission together with others from your church. It's not hard, but it does require shared commitment. Try it for a while, and after a few months reflect on your experience. You'll be surprised at how effective this simple practice can be.

Habit 4: Put Adventure Back into the Venture

Communitas involves adventure, risk, and experimentation. To experience it, churches must overcome their desire to "huddle and cuddle" and instead form around a common mission that calls them out of their burrow and into a risky adventure. This is exactly the leap of faith the twelve disciples made when they hitched their wagon to Jesus's star. And it's exactly the leap of faith groups of disciples need to make today. "Communitas isn't a warm relaxing space where you can come and go as you please. Communitas requires commitment, integrity, hard work and courage."[7]

Practice One: Take Risks

Churches can tend to be risk-averse, and yet without risk, it is highly unlikely that there will be any missional movement at all. And contrary to what we might feel at times, risk and adventure are actually good for the soul. When we encounter adventure together and have to find the inner resources to manage it, a deep form of togetherness and love is found. In such situations relationships develop into comradeship, and people encounter God in a new way.

- Keep in touch with the adaptive challenges we all face. How do we engage, communicate the gospel, and form church in a highly consumerist, post-Christian, postmodern context? Now, there's a challenge for risky endeavor. This may in fact be God's invitation to the church to rediscover itself as a missional *communitas*.[8] Brainstorm and dream of ways in which you can begin to address this challenge. Work the ideas into realistic and actionable steps.

- Use the stories in the Gospels and Acts to encourage experiences of adventure and risk.
- We are aware of a number of programs where people enroll for an overseas mission trip and then for the year following meet regularly for a meal where they reflect, pray, and encourage one another to take these experiences into everyday life.

Practice Two: Experiment

History proves that Christianity advanced because in every era there were groups of disciples who were brave enough to experiment and risk failure and ridicule. These groups formed a deep sense of camaraderie that other Christians could only dream about. While we have explored experimentation as an essential practice for pioneering and multiplying,[9] it's also a significant way to foster *communitas*.

- Create conditions in which change, adaptation, and experimentation will take place.
- Challenge the church to start thinking about how to engage an unreached group within your community. Issuing a challenge such as this will help the church learn to experiment and become more responsive to its context.
- Promote experimentation as an important task within mission. Continually experiment with new modes of church and mission.

Philosophy Cafés

There is a popular movement across the world for gathering together in third places and having good discussions on philosophy. They are known as philosophy cafés or pubs. Both Alan and Darryn have engaged in such forums and have found them exciting and fruitful contexts for mission.

Group Processing

Session 1: *Explore (talk about it)*

- If you had to highlight one idea from this section, what would it be? Why?

- In your own words, explain the idea of *communitas* to another person in the group. What ideas excite you? Concern you?

- What are the best habits and practices to consider? We have provided a few. Can you think of any others?

- What questions do you have?

- How can you imagine the group growing in this area?

Session 2: *Evaluate (reflect deeper)*

- Is *communitas* a strength or a weakness for your group?

- Does the majority of the group understand and believe in this concept?

- How is commitment to these ideas already demonstrated in your group? Give examples.

- When did the community best experience *communitas*? What were the contributing factors? What was happening at the time?

- In your opinion, what are the most important issues for creating *communitas*?

- What challenges are ahead? What are the barriers? Where do you anticipate resistance?

Session 3: *Employ (act on it)*

- What needs to happen during the next twelve months? What do you need to do that you're not currently doing?

- What will you need to let go of?

- What information and resources will you need? Who else needs to be involved?

- How will you know if you have grown in these areas? What will the key indicators be?

- What habits and practices will you seek to integrate during the next twelve months? List them here.

Action Plans

What are the first steps you will take to achieve these goals? Looking at your past, are they realistic?

What—Activity/Action	When—Date	Who—Leader/Participants
1.		
2.		
3.		
4.		

Session 4: *Personal Journal*

After processing much information, take some time to pray, listen, and respond to God. How is God prompting you, and how will you respond? Take time to record your impressions as well as insights from the group. Write a prayer expressing your desires to God. If appropriate, share your thoughts in the group, and then pray together.

- What am I sensing from God?

- What is my prayer?

Resources

Examples of Discipleship Norms

Mosaic: At Mosaic in Los Angeles, they have arranged their minimum standard for those considering involvement into four basic areas of commitment.[1]

- *A Holy Life*
  This is a pledge to life transformation. They acknowledge that everyone is imperfect but that together they will strive to live holy lives.
- *Participation in Ministry*
  This is a commitment to move beyond being a spectator. The minimum level is to meet with others for worship, be involved in a small group, and find a place of service that utilizes individual gifting.
- *Tithing*
  Every person who feels a part of Mosaic is asked to be a generous giver and tithe 10 percent of their income or more.
- *An Evangelistic Lifestyle*
  People commit to using their unique gifts and personalities to build meaningful relationships with those who don't know Christ and help others come to faith.

InnerCHANGE: A missional order dedicated to incarnating the gospel among poor communities, InnerCHANGE upholds its minimum discipleship norms with the following six commitments:[2]

- *Commitment to Humility*

  A commitment to seek to imitate the humility of Christ, who emptied himself and became a servant.
- *Commitment to Simplicity*

  A commitment to an income and lifestyle that allow each missionary to live incarnationally with the poor. A dedication to temperance in all things, and to giving joyfully and generously.
- *Commitment to Purity*

  A commitment to honesty, transparency, and fidelity in all relationships.
- *Commitment to Service*

  A commitment to compassion for the poor in words and action, to share the good news of eternal salvation, and to establish relevant expressions of Christ's kingdom among them.
- *Commitment to Community*

  A commitment to support fellow team members in prayer, love, and reconciliation, to express one's gifts as a complement to one's team members, and to love and encourage as they work to develop and use theirs.
- *Commitment to Prayer*

  In recognizing that prayer is ministry, a commitment to stillness before God, to listening before speaking, and to meditating upon God's word.

Examples of Community Mission Practices

Third Place Communities

When we think about our lifestyle and practices as a missionary community, we consider how God, the prime missionary, has acted throughout history. We acknowledge that God is always active in fulfilling his promise to re-create and make all things new. God is always *brewing* something within, among, and around us. We therefore ask "What is God brewing within, amongst, and around us?" and make the following promises:

Context	Promises	Practices	Examples
Within	TRANSFORM to become more like Jesus	Regular engagement with scripture	reading, reflection, lectio, journaling, meditation
		Daily conversation with God	examen, journaling, contemplation, confession, listening, fasting
		Action–reflection training	participate and contribute, internship, coaching, books, DVDs, seminars, intensives
		Giving financially to TPC mission	posture of giving, yearly pledge
Amongst	PARTICIPATE in Christian community	Gathering weekly with others in TPC	household, tribe, social, collective expression
		Encouragement and accountability	learning together, prayer, communion, small gatherings, confession
		Shared mission	pub, courtyard, third place rhythms, social events, community projects
		Multiplying our communities	continually identifying and developing potential for growth, starting new households, and mission
Around	CONTRIBUTE to the world by joining God in his missionary venture	Daily acts of generosity and kindness	with our things, skills, time, and money, welcoming strangers
		Weekly acts of hospitality & celebration	eating, drinking, partying, third place rhythms, rite-of-passage celebrations
		Regular meaningful engagement	sharing our faith, ongoing conversations, exploring issues, deepening relationships
		Care for the world	pursuing justice and mercy, care for creation

As you can see, these three commitments or promises begin with the letters of their name, TPC—an easy way to remember what is normative for the community. Accountability occurs by asking one simple question with three parts: "What is God brewing within, amongst, and around?" This question is asked at all levels from personal interactions, within small groups, and also in the larger gatherings.

Small Boat Big Sea

Small Boat Big Sea, a mission community located in the northern beaches of Sydney, has developed a simple order to its communal life, abbreviated with the acronym BELLS.

- **Bless**: We will bless at least one other member of our community every day.
- **Eat**: We will eat with other members of our community at least three times.
- **Listen**: we will commit ourselves weekly to listening to the promptings of God in our lives.
- **Learn**: We will read from the Gospels each week and remain diligent in learning more about Jesus.
- **Sent**: We will see our daily life as an expression of our sent-ness by God into this world.

Red

Red emerged from South Melbourne Restoration Community, which Alan led for many years. The community has recently reorganized itself into a network of missional gatherings across Melbourne, Australia. Each group in the network has covenanted to uphold a few simple common practices, which are summarized under the heading TEMPT[3] and constitute a way of expressing the values that lie at the heart of their movement.

- Together we follow

  "We commit ourselves as the people of God to live an authentic expression of Christian community." We realize that we are called to walk the journey of discipleship with others.
- Engagement with Scripture

  "We commit ourselves to constantly engage with the Holy Scripture, recognizing that it is our handbook for life." We choose to let the Bible interpret us. We recognize that the Bible is God's word and we are committed to its study. We recognize that the Bible is a book designed to be read in community.

- Mission

  "We commit ourselves to join with God in his missionary endeavor to grow the Kingdom by sharing our faith, multiplying our communities, and welcoming strangers." We believe that God's heart aches to be in relationship with His lost creation; therefore, we as his people feel compelled to communicate this love through our words and deeds, by bringing justice, showing mercy, and communicating the Gospel with the world around us.

- Passion for Jesus

  "We commit ourselves to passionately reach out to Jesus as we respond to his love for us." We have experienced the radical love of Jesus, and this fuels a passion within us to live out as his disciples in our everyday lives.

- Transformation

  "We commit ourselves to walk the road of discipleship together and to become more like Jesus every day." We are all called to follow Jesus and to strive towards growing more like the people he wants us to be. In a world of consumerism and self-interest we choose a different path. We choose to die to self in order to find true life in Jesus.

Examples of Charting APEST Results

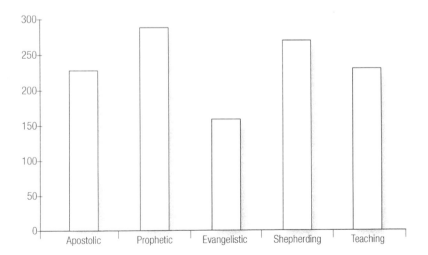

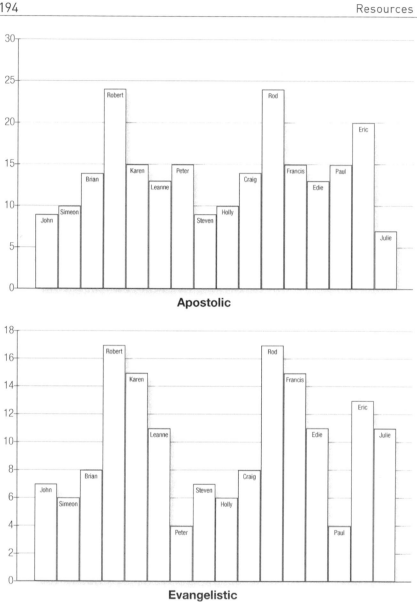

Apostolic

Evangelistic

Charting mDNA Elements

Third Place Communities used this process as a way to reflect on the mDNA elements within their mission.

	Jesus is Lord	Missional-incarnational	*Communitas*	Organic systems	Disciple making	Apostolic environment
Strength						
Weakness						
Understanding *Do the majority of people understand & believe this concept?*						
Demonstrated commitment *Give examples how commitment is demonstrated*						
When were we best at this?						
Contributing factors						
What do we need to do during the next twelve months?						
What do we need to fine tune?						
What do we need to do that we're not currently doing?						
What do we need to let go?						
What do we need that we don't have? People/resources						
How will we know if we have grown in these areas? *What will the key indicators be?*						

Example of mDNA Assessment

The following table is an example of matching habits and their related practices with the mDNA matrix. The aim of this exercise is to determine the mDNA elements each habit and practice activates. For example, the habit Organizing Community around APEST activates all six elements, while Meaningful Engagement hits only five of the six. This is a simple way to match your habits and practices with the corresponding mDNA elements, thus allowing you to assess weaknesses and strengths and to work toward streamlining your activity.

Use this as a template to create your own chart on computer, cardboard, whiteboard, or whatever is most practical. List the various habits and practices common to your church in the left-hand column, then as a group discuss and check the elements you think are activated when you engage in that particular practice. This process can be done prior to choosing a set of habits and practices or after you have been practicing them for a while. The goal is to incorporate habits and practices that activate as many of the mDNA elements as possible.

HABIT / PRACTICE	Jesus Is Lord	Missional-Incarnational	Apostolic Environment	Organic Systems	Communitas	Disciple Making
Organizing Community around APEST						
Meaningful Engagement						
Patterning Spirituality on Jesus						
Pioneering and Multiplying						
Action and Reflection						
Hallowing the Everyday						
Empowering People to Use Their Gifts						
Making the Gospels the Primary Text						

HABIT / PRACTICE	Jesus Is Lord	Missional-Incarnational	Apostolic Environment	Organic Systems	Communitas	Disciple Making
Prayer						
Developing Missionary and Discipleship Practices						
Acts of Generosity						
Shared Mission and Projects						
Catalyzing						
Hospitality						

Praying the Scriptures: The Ancient Tradition of Lectio Divina

Group Lectio Divina

1. Listening for the touch of Christ the Word
   — One person reads the text aloud (twice).
   — Silence while each repeats a word that speaks to their heart.
   — Each shares the word or phrase with the group (no elaboration).

2. How Christ the Word speaks to me
   — Another person reads the text once more.
   — Silence for two minutes, reflecting on "Where does the reading touch my life today?"
   — Each briefly shares with the group. "I hear, I see. . ."

3. What Christ the Word invites me to do
   — Third reading by another person.
   — Silence for two minutes. Reflection on "I believe God wants me to _____ today/this week."
   — Share aloud the results of each person's reflection.
   — After full sharing, pray for the person on your right.

Individual Lectio Divina

Find a comfortable place, and begin to concentrate on your breathing, focusing on the air moving in your nostrils and out your mouth. Listen to the sounds of the world around you as you slow down for a time of contemplation.

1. Reading: *lectio*
   — Slowly read a text to yourself.
   — Repeat the parts of the text that speak to the depths of your heart. Linger on portions of the text that seem to speak to you in a special way.

2. Meditation: *meditatio*
   — Consider a phrase or word, allowing it to infiltrate your thoughts.
   — What do the words mean for me now?

3. Prayer: *oratio*
   — Offer yourself, your thoughts, and the word to God.
   — Enter into conversation with God.
   — What do I need to change?

4. Contemplation: *contemplatio*
   — Rest silently in God's presence, communicating with the One who inspired the scriptures.

The Six Thinking Hats of Edward de Bono

The six hats represent six modes of thinking and are directions to think rather than labels for thinking. That is, the hats are used proactively rather than reactively. The method promotes fuller input from more people. In de Bono's words, it "separates ego from performance." Everyone is able to contribute to the exploration without denting egos, as they are just using the yellow hat or red hat (or whatever hat). The six-hats system encourages performance rather than ego defense. People can contribute under any hat, even though they initially support the opposite view. The key point is that a hat is a direction to think, rather than a label for thinking.

1. **White Hat:** Think of white paper. It's neutral and carries information. The White Hat has to do with data and information. The White Hat asks what information we have here. What information is missing? What information would we like to have? How are we going to get that information?

2. **Red Hat:** Think of red and fire and warmth. This has to do with feelings, intuition, hunches, and emotions. "Putting on my red hat, this is what I feel: _____." "My gut feeling is _____." "My intuition tells me prices will soon fall."

3. **Black Hat:** Think of the stern judge wearing black robes who comes down heavily on wrongdoers. This is the caution hat. Prevents us from making mistakes, making decisions hastily, doing silly things, illegal things, etc. It points out why something cannot be done or why something will not work.

4. **Yellow Hat:** Think of sunshine. The yellow hat is for optimism and the positive view. This looks for feasibility and how something can be done. It looks for benefits—but they must be logically based. "That might work if we/I _____."

5. **Green Hat:** Think of vegetation and rich growth. The green hat is for creative thinking, for new ideas, additional alternatives, putting forward possibilities and hypotheses. This requires creative effort. "We need some new ideas here." "Are there any alternatives? Don't worry how bizarre they might sound at first." "Could we do this differently?" "Could there be another explanation?"

6. **Blue Hat:** Think of the sky and an overview. This is for process control. The Blue Hat thinks about the thinking being used. It sets the agenda for thinking. It suggests the next step in the thinking. The blue hat can ask for other hats. It asks for summaries, conclusions, and decisions. It can make comments when you have it on: "Could we summarize how far we have got?" "I think we should look at the priorities." "I suggest we try some more green-hat thinking now." This is usually for the chairperson or organizer of the meeting.

Movies to Watch for *Communitas*

- *Band of Brothers*
- *Identity, The Bourne Supremacy,* and *The Bourne Ultimatum*
- *The Lord of the Rings* trilogy
- *Finding Nemo*
- *Master and Commander*
- *The Matrix* trilogy
- *Saving Private Ryan*
- *Toy Story*
- *The Wizard of Oz*

Vital
Online Resources for the *Application* of
THE FORGOTTEN WAYS

mPULSE. This online test is designed to help identify and "measure" the presence of Apostolic Genius (comprised of the six elements of mDNA) in your church. *mPULSE* (missional pulse) is designed to take the pulse of churches adopting the movement style approach to church and mission described in *The Forgotten Ways*. It will help in both assessing the "missionality" of the organization, as well as provide a strategic tool for the development of Apostolic Genius as you apply the model. Do it once a year to take the pulse of your church/organization. Go to www.theforgottenways.org/mpulse.

APEST test: Similarly, in order to fully develop a missional type ministry in your church and/or organization, we have developed the online *APEST test*. This allows you and your team to assess (and develop) Ephesians 4:11 ministry in your midst. There are both individual tests as well as 360° feedback tests to identify where each individual is located within the *APEST* profile. Go to www.theforgottenways.org/apest.

You can also engage in *blog* conversations with Alan and others on www.theforgottenways.org

Glossary of Key Terms

In order to assist the reader with some of the more technical words and phrases, this glossary has been adopted from *The Forgotten Ways*. Essentially, it is a set of definitions that are key to understanding the book.

Adaptive challenge

A concept deriving from chaos theory. Adaptive challenges are situations where a living system faces the challenge to find a new reality. Adaptive challenges come from two possible sources: a situation of (1) significant threat or (2) compelling opportunity. The threat poses an "adapt or die" scenario on the organism or organization. The compelling opportunity might simply come as "the food is better in the next valley . . . let's move!" type scenario. Adaptive challenges set the context for innovation and adaptation.

Adaptive leadership

An adaptive leader is the type of leader who develops learning organizations and manages to help the organization transition into different forms or expression where agility, responsiveness, innovation, and entrepreneurship are needed. Adaptive leaders are needed in times of significant threat or considerable new opportunity, or both. This has direct relevance to our situation at the dawn of the twenty-first century. Compare to *operational leadership* below.

APEST

The term I use to describe the fivefold ministry formula in Ephesians 4. APEST is an acronym for Apostle, Prophet, Evangelist, Shepherd, Teacher.

This has been adapted to APEST for the profiling mechanism found on www.theforgottenways.org/apest.

Apostolic

I use the term very specifically to describe not so much the theology of the church but the mode of the New Testament church—to describe something of its energy, impulse, and genius as well as its leadership structures.

Apostolic Genius

Apostolic Genius is the phrase I developed to try to conceive and articulate that unique energy and force that imbues phenomenal Jesus movements in history. My own conclusions are that Apostolic Genius is made up of six components (perhaps more, never less). Five are what I call mDNA and the other has to do with its spirituality and theology. For the most part, I focus on the five elements of mDNA when I use the term. The five elements are missional-incarnational impulse, apostolic environment, disciple-making, organic systems, and *communitas*. Loaded into the term *Apostolic Genius* is the full combination of all the elements of mDNA that together form a constellation, as it were, each shedding light on the others. I also believe it is latent, or embedded, into the very nature of God's gospel people. I suggest that when all the elements of mDNA are present and are in dynamic relationship with the other elements, and an adaptive challenge acts as a catalyst, then Apostolic Genius is activated.

Attractional church

Essentially, attractional church operates from the assumption that to bring people to Jesus we need to first bring them to church. It also describes the type or mode of engagement that was birthed during the Christendom period of history, when the church was perceived as being a central institution of society and therefore expected people to "come and hear the gospel" rather than taking a "go-to-them" type of mentality. Not to be confused with being culturally attractive.

Biblical Hebraic

Describes the worldview that basically formed, framed, and sustains the biblical revelation. Refers to the Hebraic worldview specifically found in the scriptures. *Hebraic* on its own can encompass the insights of later Judaism as well.

Chaos and chaos theory

Chaos theory is a new scientific discipline that seeks to explore the nature of living systems and how they respond to their environment. Thus, it applies not only to organisms but also to human organizations, which are considered living systems that operate in a very similar way to organic life. In the light of living systems, chaos is not necessarily a negative thing but can be the context for significant innovation. However, it does pose a threat to living systems that fail to respond appropriately to the conditions of chaos. See chapters 3 and 7 for explorations into these ideas.

Christendom

Describes the standardized form and expression of the church and mission formed in the post-Constantine period (312 AD to present). It is important to note that was not the original form in which the church expressed itself. The Christendom church is fundamentally different from the NT church, which is made up of a network of grassroots missional communities organized as a movement. Christendom is marked by the following characteristics:

1. Its mode of engagement is attractional as opposed to missional/sending. It assumes a certain centrality of the church in relation to its surrounding culture. (The missional church is a "going/sending one" and operates in the incarnational mode.)
2. A shift of focus to dedicated, sacred buildings/places of worship. The association of buildings with *church* fundamentally altered the way the church perceived itself. It became more static and institutional in form. (The early church had no recognized dedicated buildings other than houses, shops, etc.)
3. The emergence of an institutionally recognized, professional clergy class acting primarily in a pastor-teacher mode. (In the NT church people were commissioned into leadership by local churches or by an apostolic leader. But this was basically different from a denominational or institutional ordination we know in Christendom. This had the effect of breaking up the people of God into the professional Christian and the lay Christian. The idea of a separated clergy, I maintain, is alien to an NT church, as it is in the Jesus movements of the early church and China.)
4. The paradigm is also characterized by the institutionalization of grace in the form of sacraments administered by an institutionally authorized priesthood. (The NT church's form of communion was an actual [daily?] meal dedicated to Jesus in the context of everyday life and the home.)

Christocentric

Simply that Christ is center. If something is Christocentric, then its organizing principle is the person and work of Christ.

Christology/Christological

Essentially Christology comprises the biblical teaching of and about Jesus the Messiah. For instance, when I say Christology must inform all aspects of the church's life and work, it means that Jesus must be first and foremost in our life and self-definition as church and disciple. The adjectival form simply means that the element being described must be referenced primarily by our understanding and experience of Jesus the Messiah.

Church Planting

The initiation and development of new, organic, missional-incarnational, communities of faith in multiple contexts. We affirm that all true mission aims at the development of communities of faith. Thus church planting is an essential part of any authentic missional strategy.

Communitas

Adopted from the work of anthropologist Victor Turner, who used the term to describe the experiences that were part of initiation ceremonies of young African boys (see *liminality*.) The related ideas of liminality and *communitas*, one of the key elements of mDNA, describe the dynamics of the Christian community inspired to overcome their instincts to "huddle and cuddle," and to instead form themselves around a common mission that calls them onto a dangerous journey to unknown places, a mission that calls the church to shake off its collective securities and to plunge into the world of action. There they will experience disorientation and marginalization but also encounter God and one another in a new way. *Communitas* is therefore always linked with the experience of liminality. It involves adventure and movement, and it describes that unique experience of *togetherness* that really happens only among a group of people inspired by the vision of a better world actually attempting to do something about it.

Complexity

Complexity is related to a situation of chaos. In essence living systems theory maintains that living organisms tend to organize themselves in greater degrees of complexity. Complexity also acknowledges that when we are dealing with living systems, they are indeed complex. Because of complexity, relatively small actions can have significant consequences in the system.

Constantinianism

This is another word for Christendom, because Christendom was basically initiated by Constantine's actions in bringing the church into official relationship with the state. Constantinianism is the type of all modes of church that resulted from the merger between church and state and has dominated our mind-sets for the last seventeen centuries.

Cultural Distance

A concept that helps us try and assess just how far a people group is from a *meaningful* engagement with the gospel. To do this we have to view this as something of a continuum that looks like this. . . .

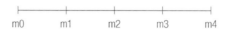

Each numeral with the prefix *m* indicates *one significant cultural barrier to the meaningful communication of the gospel.* An obvious example of such a barrier would be language. If you have to reach across a language barrier, you have a problem. But others could be race, history, religion/worldview, culture, etc. For instance, in Islamic contexts, the gospel has struggled to make any significant inroads because religion, race, and history make a meaningful engagement with the gospel very difficult indeed. Because of the Crusades, the Christendom church really damaged the capacity for Muslim people to apprehend Christ, and Semitic peoples have long memories. So we might put mission to Islamic people in an m3 to m4 situation (religion, history, language, race, and culture). The same is true for the Jewish people in the West. It is very hard to "speak meaningfully" in either of these situations.

Dualism (Particularly Platonic Dualism)

The view that spirit is good and that anything that resists spirit is necessarily bad. Matter resists spirit and is therefore evil. The form that really impacted the church came from Plato. Plato believed that the *real* world was in fact the world of eternal ideas and essences located in an invisible spiritual reality, and that the world of matter and things is but its shadow and therefore has no essential reality. A shadow is only a reflection of the real and not the real itself. The real was to be found in its essence of an object, in the Idea of it, and not in the way it appears to us in our world. This has also been called dualism, and by the fifth century AD it had become the predominant worldview in the Western church. Dualism thus naturally leans toward *essence* over *function*. The reality of a thing abides in its idea or essence and not in its appearance nor in what it does. The net effect of this doctrine was to divide the world between the sacred or the essential, and secular or the functional/physical. This has massive ramifications for the way we do church and structure our spirituality.

Early Church

The period of the history of the church spanning the New Testament church as well as that up to the time of Constantine in 312 AD. The way I use the term implies a certain type or mode of the church: that of a radical, grassroots network of churches and people, organized as a movement, largely in the context of persecution.

Ecclesia

The predominant biblical word translated as "church" in English. The way I use it in this book will highlight something of the pristine idea of the church as God intended it.

Ecclesiology

Classically, this refers to the biblical teaching about the church.

Emergence

"The principle of *emergence* was developed to explain the ways organisms develop and adapt in differing environments. Contrary to popular notions that they develop through some top-down, pre-determined, well planned strategy, *emergence theory* shows that complex systems develop from the bottom up. Relatively simple clusters of cells, or groups of individuals, who individually don't know how to address a complex challenge, when they come together will form, out of relatively simple interactions, an organizational culture of a higher complexity that can address these challenges. In other words, the answers to the challenges faced by organisms and organizations in changing environments tend to emerge from the bottom up rather than get planned beforehand from the top down. This is why we describe missional leadership as *the cultivation of environments within which the missional imagination of the people of God might emerge.*"[1]

Emerging Missional Church (EMC)

Essentially I developed the term to identify and describe the new form of *ecclesia* forming in our day. In the way that it is used in this book, it will be viewed as an emergent structure, a new form of *ecclesia* in our day. As such it is not just emerging or missional, but it is the combination of these two factors that has created a new form of church. I also use it to describe the phenomenal movement that is going on in our day. This is not to deny the continuity of the EMC with the people of God in all ages, but to distinguish it in form alone.

Evangelistic-attractional

This describes the missional impulse of the Christendom church and that of the church growth movement. Essentially, it involves the assumption that all outreach and evangelism must bring people back to church in order to facilitate the numerical growth of that church. Another way to say it is "outreach and in-drag." The way I use it is to pose it as the opposite of the missional-incarnational impulse.

Environments/Fields

The universe in which we live is filled with unseen fields. Though invisible, fields nonetheless assert a definite influence on objects within their orbit. There are gravitational fields, electromagnetic fields, quantum fields, etc., which form part of the very structure of reality. These unseen influences affect the behavior of atoms, objects, and people. But fields don't just exist in nature and physics; they exist in social systems as well. For example, think about the power of ideas in human affairs—a powerful idea has no substance, but one cannot doubt its influence. Note too the power of good and evil on people and societies. I use this idea to try and communicate that leadership itself creates an invisible field wherein certain behaviors take place. To try to conceptualize leadership as influence, think of a magnet and its effect on iron filings scattered on a sheet of paper. When the filings come into the orbit of influence of the magnet, they form a certain pattern that we all recognize from our school days. I think leadership does exactly the same thing—it creates a *field*, which in turn influences people in a certain way, just as the magnet influences the iron filings.

Fitness Landscape

Essentially, a context that tests the fitness of a living system, be it an organism or an organization.

Hebraic

Refer to *Biblical Hebraic* above. Essentially, the worldview nurtured primarily by the Bible. *Hebraic* in the broader sense can also mean the worldview of the Jewish people as a racial group, deeply influenced as it is by Judaism.

Hellenism

The way it is used in this book is as a contrast to Hebraic thinking. Hellenism is the ideologies that shaped and informed the Greek worldview. Together with Roman ideas it formed the basis of the worldview of the Roman Empire, and as the church moved further away from its Hebraic roots, Hellenism became the predominant worldview of the Christendom church.

Incarnational

The incarnation refers to the act of God in entering into the created universe and realm of human affairs as the man Jesus of Nazareth. When we talk of *incarnational* in relation to mission, it means similarly embodying the culture and life of a target group in order to meaningfully reach that group of people from within their culture. I also use the term to describe the missionary act of *going* to a target people group as opposed to the invitation to come to our cultural group in order to hear the gospel.

Institution and Institutionalism

Institutions are organizations initially set up in order to fill a necessary religious and social function and to provide some sort of structural support for whatever that function needs. In many ways this is the very purpose of structure, as organizations are needed if we seek to act collectively for common cause, for example, the original purpose of denominations. The problem happens when institutions move beyond being mere structural support and become a governing body of sorts. My working definition of institutionalization is that it occurs *when we outsource an essentially grassroots/local function to a centralized structure/organization. Over time the centralized structure tends to become depersonalized and becomes restrictive of deviating behavior and freedom.* In other words, it occurs when in the name of some convenience we get others to do what we must do ourselves. When this happens there is a transfer of responsibility and power/authority to the governing body. In this situation it inevitably becomes a locus of power that uses some of that power to sanction behaviors of its members that are out of keeping with the institution. It becomes a power to itself and begins to assert a kind of restrictive authority on nonconforming behaviors. The problem exaggerates when over time power is entrenched in the institution and it creates a culture of restraint. No one intends this in the first place; it seems to be just of our fallen human condition in relation to power. When institutions get to this point, they are extremely hard to change. Seen in this light, all great innovators and thinkers are rebels against institutionalism. We often see portrayals of the institution of the Roman Catholic Church on TV and in movies that highlight how oppressive religious institutionalism can get. And while these are sometimes a caricature, make no mistake there is real historical substance to this portrayal. Most non-Christian people in the West view most churches as repressive institutions, with some justification.

Jesus Movements

When I refer to Jesus movements (or substitute this term with "phenomenal Christian or apostolic movements), I am primarily referring to the two test cases I have adopted, namely, those of the early church and the Chinese underground church. But the phrase also refers to those other amazing movements in history where exponential growth and impact occurred, for example, Wesley's revival or Third World Pentecostalism today.

Leadership Matrix

The term for apostolic, prophetic, evangelistic, pastoral, and didactic (teaching) leadership as it is drawn from the ministry matrix (see below and APEST). Viewed as such, leadership is a *calling within a calling*.

Liminality

Liminality comes from the word *liminal*, which describes a boundary or threshold situation. In the way that it is used in this book, it describes the contexts or condition from which *communitas* can emerge. Situations of liminality can be extreme, where the participant is literally cast out of the normal structures of life, is humbled, disoriented, and subjected to various rites of passage, which together constitute a form of test as to whether the participant will be allowed back into society and to transition to the next level in the prevailing social structure. Liminality therefore applies to that situation where people find themselves in an in-between, marginal state in relation to the surrounding society, a place of danger and disorientation.

mDNA

I have inserted the m to the letters *DNA* purely to differentiate it from the biological version—it simply means *missional*DNA. What DNA does for biological systems, mDNA does for ecclesial ones. DNA in biological life

- is found in all living cells,
- codes genetic information for the transmission of inherited traits beyond that of the initiating organism,
- is self-replicating, and
- carries vital information for healthy reproduction.

mDNA therefore does the same for the church as God has designed it. And with this concept/metaphor I hope to explain why the presence of a simple intrinsic, reproducible, central guiding mechanism is necessary for the reproduction and sustainability of genuine missional movements. As an organism holds together, and each cell understands its function in relation to its DNA, so the church in given contexts finds its reference point in its built-in mDNA.

Memes and Memeplex

Essentially, a meme is to the world of ideas what genes are to the world of biology—they encode ideas in easily reproducible form. In this theory, a memeplex is a complex of memes (ideas) that constitute the inner structure of an ideology or a belief system. And like DNA, it seeks to replicate itself by mutation into evolving forms of ideas by adding, developing, or shedding memes as the situation requires. Sounds strange, doesn't it? Why this idea is so valuable is that the memeplex has the capacity to reproduce itself by embedding itself in the receiver's brain and passing itself on from there to other brains via human communication. We all know the feeling of being captivated by an idea, don't we? We get caught up into its life. In some way that is exactly the way we all got caught up into the gospel and so adopted a biblical worldview.

Ministry matrix

This term is used to describe the ministry callings of the church in terms of the teaching of Ephesians 4:7ff., namely, that the whole church is comprised of people who are apostolic, prophetic, evangelistic, pastoral, and didactic (teaching). Ephesians 4:7 indicates that "to *each one* is given," and 4:11 says, "It was he who gave *some* to be apostles, *some* to be prophets, *some* to be evangelists, and *some* to be pastors and teachers." Therefore, the term *ministry matrix* applies the APEST model to the *whole* church and not just its leadership as per the more common interpretation (cf. *leadership matrix*).

Missiology/Missiological

Missiology is the study of missions. As a discipline, it seeks to identify the primal impulses in the scriptures that compel God's people into engagement with the world. Such impulses involve, for example, the *missio Dei* (the mission of God), the Incarnation, and the kingdom of God. It also describes the authentic church's commitment to social justice, relational righteousness, and evangelism. As such missiology seeks to define the church's purposes in light of God's will for the world. It also seeks to study the methods of achieving these ends, both from scripture and from history. The term *missiological* simply draws off these meanings.

Missional

A favorite term: I use it to describe a certain type or mode of church, leadership, Christianity, etc. For example, a *missional* church is one whose primary commitment is to the missionary calling of the people of God.

Missional leadership is that form of leadership that emphasizes the primacy of the missionary calling of God's people, etc.

Missional Church

Missional church is a church that defines itself, and organizes its life around, its real purpose as an agent of God's mission to the world. In other words, the church's true and authentic organizing principle is mission. When the church is in mission, it is the true church. The church itself not only is a product of that mission, but is obligated and destined to extend it by whatever means possible. The mission of God flows directly through every believer and every community of faith that adheres to Jesus. To obstruct this is to block God's purposes in and through his people.

Missional ecclesiology

Similar to above, the area of study that explores the nature of the Christian movements, and therefore the church, as they are shaped by Jesus and his mission. The attention is chiefly on how the church organizes and expresses itself when mission is the central focus.

Missional-Incarnational

A phrase I have coined to try describe the impetus that is part of significant Jesus movements in history. In putting the two words together, I hope to link the two practices that in essence form one and the same action. Namely, *missional* . . . the outgoing thrust of the Jesus movements, like the scattering of seeds or of the dispersion of bacteria in a sneeze. It is an essential aspect of Christianity's capacity to spread itself and cross cultural boundaries. It is linked to the theology of the *missio Dei* (the mission of God), where God *sends* his Son and we ourselves become a *sent* people. The incarnational side of the equation relates to the embedding and deepening of the gospel and church into host cultures. It will mean that in order to relate to and influence the host group, it will need to do it from within its cultural forms and expressions. This is linked directly to the Incarnation of God in Jesus.

Mode

Another favorite word, it simply describes the method, style, or manner of that which it refers to. The online Encarta dictionary defines *mode* as "a way, manner, or form, for example, a way of doing something, or the form in which something exists." Thus, the mode of the early church describes its methodology, its stance, its approach to the world, etc.

Movement

In this book I use the term sociologically to describe the organizational structures and ethos of the missional church. I believe that the NT church was itself a movement and not an institution (cf. *institution/institutionalism*, above). I believe that to be genuinely missional, a church must always strive to maintain a movement style and ethos.

Operational Leadership

Essentially, operational leadership is that type suited for organizations that are in relatively stable environments where maintenance and development of current programming constitute the core tasks of leadership. This form of leadership is built on the assumptions of social engineering and is thus built squarely on a mechanistic view of the world. It works, and is appropriate for *some* organizations: those who find themselves in situations of stability. Operational leadership works best when the problems faced can be dealt with by drawing upon a preexisting repertoire and are exploited with more speed, quality, or scale. It is usually a top-down form of leadership, where a solution is devised from above and rolled out through the ranks. If an organization requires downsizing, restructuring, or reducing costs, if sharpened execution is the key to success, then operational leadership *is* probably the best bet.

Strange Attractors

In living systems theory there exists a phenomenon called the "strange attractor." Essentially, strange attractors are that force, analogous to a compass, or an animal's deep instinct, which orients a living system in one particular direction and provides organisms with the impetus to migrate out of their comfort zone.[2] They are found in all living systems, including human organizations. As has been discussed in the chapter on chaos theory, a system that is in equilibrium is inevitably in decline and to become adaptive needs to move toward the edge of chaos to initiate its latent capacity to adapt and therefore survive. As in biological systems, the role of the strange attractor in organizations as living systems is therefore critical to the ability of the organization to survive an adaptive challenge.

Notes

A Note to Leaders

1. It is important that leadership understand the dynamics of change. A book that takes change processes seriously in relation to missional church is *The Missional Leader: Equipping Your Church to Reach a Changing World* (San Francisco: Jossey-Bass, 2006) by Alan Roxburgh and Fred Romanuk.

2. The Missional Test is available at www.theforgottenways.org.

3. This very useful phrase is borrowed from the authors of *Surfing the Edge of Chaos,* 14.

Chapter 1 Introduction to the Forgotten Ways

1. For a definition of Christendom, see the glossary. The nature, history, and structure of Christendom is more fully explored in chapter 2.

2. Rodney Stark is considered to be the authority on these issues, and in his book called *The Rise of Christianity* he suggests an array of possible answers ranging from conservative to broad estimates. I have tried to average these estimates (according to Stark, between 40 and 50 percent, exponentially per decade) and compare this with other sources. These are my findings. See R. Stark, *The Rise of Christianity: How the Obscure, Marginal Jesus Movement Became the Dominant Religious Force in the Western World in a Few Centuries* (San Francisco: HarperCollins, 1996), 6–13.

3. See glossary.

4. Philip Yancey, "Discreet and Dynamic: Why, with No Apparent Resources, Chinese Churches Thrive," *Christianity Today* 48 (July 2004): 72.

5. Another remarkable movement, one that changed the destiny of Europe and beyond, was the Celtic Movement. While it is out of the scope of this book to explore the nature of the Irish mission to the West, many similarities remain to that of the early church as well as the Chinese church.

6. Stephen Addison, *Movement Dynamics, Keys to the Expansion and Renewal of the Church in Mission* (unpublished manuscript), 5.

Chapter 2 The Heart of It All

1. Michael Frost and Alan Hirsch, *The Shaping of Things to Come* (Peabody, MA: Hendrickson, 2003).

2. Michael Frost and Alan Hirsch, *ReJesus* (Peabody, MA: Hendrickson, 2008).

3. Nashville: Thomas Nelson, 1995.

4. New York: HarperOne, 1998

5. Grand Rapids: Eerdmans, 1983.

6. Grand Rapids: Brazos, 2006.

7. http://www.ntwrightonline.com/.

8. New York: Crossroad/Faith and Formation, 1993.

9. http://mdei.wordpress.com/core-practices. Based in the city of Melbourne, Australia.

10. These ideas are summarized from Michael Frost and Alan Hirsch, *The Shaping of Things To Come* (Peabody, MA: Hendrickson, 2003), 124–25.

11. Michael Frost, *Exiles: Living Missionally in a Post-Christian Culture* (Peabody, MA: Hendrickson, 2006), 311–14.

12. Summarized from Frost and Hirsch, *Shaping of Things to Come,* 128–29.

13. Frost and Hirsch, *ReJesus.*

14. For more information, see http://en.wikipedia.org/wiki/Stations_of_the_Cross.

15. Downers Grove, IL: InterVarsity Press, 2002.

Chapter 3 Disciple Making

1. Neil Cole, *Organic Church* (San Francisco: Jossey Bass, 2007), 26.

2. Matthew 28:18–20.

3. Romans 8:29; 2 Corinthians 3:18.

4. Erwin Raphael McManus, *An Unstoppable Force* (Loveland, CO: Group, 2001), 212.

5. Ibid., 202, 203.

6. Darrell L. Guder, *Treasure in Clay Jars, Patterns in Missional Faithfulness,* Lois Y. Barrett, gen. ed., (Grand Rapids: Eerdmans, 2004), 69, 70.

7. Ibid., 62.

8. 2 Timothy 3:16–17.

9. This is known as Lectio Divina; for an example, see the resource section at the end of this book.

10. For more details on Edward DeBono's Six Thinking Hats, see the resource section at the end of this book.

11. Quote taken from editorial review, http://www.amazon.com/dp/0310271053.

12. To see an example of Examen, go to the resource section at the end of this book.

13. 1 Corinthians 12:12–31.

14. Ephesians 4:16.

15. John 13:34–35.

16. www.smallboatbigsea.org.

17. Bless, Eat, Listen, Learn, Sent.

18. www.smallboatbigsea.org/dna.

19. For an example of lectio and examen, please see the resource section in this book.

20. You can find more information at http://cmaresources.org.

21. E-mail nsw@forge.org.au for information on acquiring Exilio.

22. See www.shapevine.com.

23. Luke 9:1–2.

24. Ephesians 4:11–12.

25. Romans 12:6–8; 1 Corinthians 12:18.

26. While this test is based on the APEST gifts in Ephesians 4, there are other lists mentioned in Romans 12:6–8 and 1 Corinthians 12:12–31, which we suggest you also explore as a community.

27. Deuteronomy 6:4–7.

28. Steve's new book *TransforMissional Coaching: Empowering Missional Leaders in a Changing Ministry World* (Nashville: B&H Books, 2008) develops the system described above.

Chapter 4 The Missional-Incarnational Impulse

1. Ash Barker from UNOH suggested this in a presentation during a Forge Mission Training event.

2. Matthew 28:19.

3. Third places are social contexts beyond the home or workplace such as sporting groups, pubs, cafés, clubs, etc.

4. Michael Frost and Alan Hirsch, *The Shaping of Things to Come* (Peabody, MA: Hendrickson, 2003), 64.

5. We applaud many new mission groups who have sought to engage the community in mission. Nevertheless, while some have done well in connecting, many have created reasonably complicated and time-consuming approaches. Our concern is that it's tempting to spend too much time on the outward movement, leaving little time and energy for deepening relationships.

6. Michael Frost, mission seminar, Hobart, Tasmania, March 1, 2008.

7. Frost and Hirsch, *Shaping of Things to Come,* 25.

8. Darrell Guder, *The Incarnation and the Church's Witness* (Valley Forge, PA: Trinity, 1999), 22.

9. Colossians 4:5–6.

10. 1 Peter 3:15b.

11. Frost and Hirsch, *Shaping of Things to Come,* 100–107.

12. Ecclesiastes 3:11b.

13. Matthew 5:16.

14. 1 Peter 2:12.

15. Philippians 2:15.

16. Matthew 11:19.

17. Frost and Hirsch, *Shaping of Things to Come.*

18. There is more information on starting new mission within the Apostolic Environment section.

Chapter 5 Apostolic Environment

1. Multiplication will also be explored within organic systems.

2. Ori Brafman, Rod Beckstrom, *The Starfish and the Spider: The Unstoppable Power of Leaderless Organizations* (New York: Portfolio, 2006).

3. Malcolm Gladwell, *The Tipping Point* (Boston: Back Bay Books, 2002).

4. Of the many leaders we have met who have undergone formal ministry training, few have been schooled in the art of shaping culture. We mention this because knowing how to shape a missionary culture is an integral role for which most current leaders will need to develop their capacity.

5. SWOT stands for strengths, weaknesses, opportunities, and threats.

6. Ashley Barker, *Surrender All: A Call to Submerge with Christ* (Melbourne: UNOH, 2005), 159.

7. Ibid., 160.

8. Ibid.

9. "First places" refers to the home environment.

10. See the resource section at the end of the book for an example of these Excel charts.

11. www.forge.org.au; www.shapevine.com; www.missio.us; www.epochcenter.org; www .ecclesianet.org; www.mtnetwork.ca; www.allelon.org/main.cfm; www.dawneurope.net.

12. Dee Hock, *The Birth of the Chaordic Age* (San Francisco: Berrett-Koehler, 1999) quoted in *The Forgotten Ways,* 149.

13. Idea summarized from Brafman and Beckstrom, *The Starfish and the Spider,* 91–94.

14. Ibid.

15. Ibid., 130.

Chapter 6 Organic Systems

1. *Forgotten Ways,* 195.

2. See, for instance, George Hunter III, *The Celtic Way of Evangelism: How Christianity Can Reach the West . . . Again* (Nashville: Abingdon, 2000).

3. www.christianassociates.org/index.

4. *Forgotten Ways,* 190.

5. *The Missional Leader: Equipping Your Church to Reach a Changing World* (San Francisco: Jossey-Bass, 2006).

6. Dee Hock, *The Birth of the Chaordic Age* (San Francisco: Berrett-Koehler, 1999).

7. Idea from Richard Karash.

8. Hock, *Birth of the Chaordic Age.*

9. The question is "What is Jesus brewing *within, amongst* and *around*?"

10. Dee Hock, *One From Many: Visa and the Rise of Chaordic Organization* (San Francisco: Berrett-Koehler), 233–34.

11. Stephen Covey, *The Seven Habits of Highly Effective People* (New York: Simon & Schuster, 2004). The habits are: *seek first to understand and then be understood, seek win-win,* and *synergy*.

12. Ibid., 34–35.

13. This information is gleaned from http://www.wikisummaries.org/The_Tipping _Point.

14. Taken from the book by Chip and Dan Heath *Made to Stick: Why Some Ideas Survive and Others Die* (New York: Random House, 2007).

Chapter 7 *Communitas,* Not Community

1. See Victor Turner, *The Ritual Process* (Ithaca, NY: Cornell University Press, 1969); and Victor Turner, "Passages, Margins, and Poverty: Religious Symbols of Communitas," part 1, *Worship* 46, nos. 7 and 8.

2. From Church of the Savior in Washington.

3. Michael Frost, *Exiles: Living Missionally in a Post-Christian Culture* (Peabody, MA: Hendrickson), 2006.

4. Michael Frost and Alan Hirsch, *The Shaping of Things to Come* (Peabody, MA: Hendrickson, 2003), 27–28.

5. "Missional-Incarnational" chapter.

6. *Forgotten Ways*, 226–27.

7. Frost, *Exiles*, 115.

8. *Forgotten Ways*, 222.

9. Mentioned in the "Apostolic Environment" chapter

Resources

1. Erwin Raphael McManus, *An Unstoppable Force* (Sydney: Strand, 2006), 216.

2. This is a summarized version; the complete list can be found at http://www.innerchange.org/commitments.

3. See http://www.red.org.au/Reserved_Philosophy_Only.html.

Glossary of Key Terms

1. A. Roxburgh and F. Romanuk, "Christendom Thinking ," 28.

2. Pascale, Millemann and Gioja, *Surfing the Edge of Chaos*, 69.

Recommended Reading

Addison, S. B. "A Basis for the Continuing Ministry of the Apostle in the Church's Mission," D.Min. diss., Fuller Theological Seminary, 1995.

———. "Movement Dynamics, Keys to the Expansion and Renewal of the Church in Mission" (unpublished manuscript, 2003).

Adeney, D. H. *China: The Church's Long March* (Ventura, CA: Regal, 1985).

Arquilla, J., and D. Ronfeldt. *Networks and Netwars: The Future of Terror, Crime, and Militancy* (downloadable online resource, available at www.rand.org/publications/MR/MR1382/).

Barker, A., and J. Hayes. *Sub-Merge: Living Deep in a Shallow World* (Springvale, VIC, Aus.: GO Alliance, 2002).

Barrett, C. K. *The Signs of an Apostle* (Carlisle: Paternoster, 1996).

Borden, P. D. *Hit the Bullseye: How Denominations Can Aim the Congregation at the Mission Field* (Nashville: Convergence, 2003).

Bosch, D. *Transforming Mission: Paradigm Shifts in the Theology of Mission* (Maryknoll, NY: Orbis, 1991).

Breen, M., and W. Kallestad. *The Passionate Church: The Art of Life-Changing Discipleship* (Colorado Springs: Nexgen, 2004).

Brewin, K. *The Complex Christ: The Signs of Emergence in the Urban Church* (London: SPCK, 2004).

Cahill, T. *How the Irish Saved Civilization: The Untold Story of Ireland's Heroic Role from the Fall of Rome to the Rise of Medieval Europe* (New York: Anchor, 1995).

Capra, F. *The Hidden Connections: A Science for Sustainable Living* (London: HarperCollins, 2002).

————. *The Turning Point: Science, Society, and the Rising Culture* (London: Flamingo, 1982).

————. *The Web of Life* (New York: Anchor, 1996).

Carnell, C. *Bright Shadow of Reality* (Grand Rapids: Eerdmans, 1974).

Castells, M., *The Rise of the Network Society*, 2nd ed. (Oxford: Blackwell, 2000).

Christensen, C. M. *Seeing What's Next: Using the Theories of Innovation to Predict Industry Change* (Cambridge: Harvard Business School Press, 2004).

Cole, N. *Cultivating a Life for God: Multiplying Disciples through Life Transformation Groups* (Elgin, IL: Brethren Press, 1999).

————. *Organic Church: Growing Faith Where Life Happens* (San Francisco: Jossey-Bass, 2005).

Collins, J. *Good to Great: Why Some Companies Make the Leap, and Others Don't* (New York: HarperBusiness, 2001).

Dale, T. and F. *Simply Church* (Manchaca, TX: Karis, 2002).

Daniel-Rops, H. *The Church of Apostles and Martyrs* (New York: Image, 1962).

de Bono, E. *New Thinking for a New Millennium* (St. Ives, NSW, Aus.: Viking, 1999), ix.

Easum, B. *Unfreezing Moves: Following Jesus into the Mission Field* (Nashville: Abingdon, 2001).

Friedman, M. *Martin Buber: The Life of Dialogue* (New York: Harper & Row, 1960).

Frost, M., and A. Hirsch. *The Shaping of Things to Come: Innovation and Mission for the 21st-Century Church* (Peabody, MA: Hendrickson, 2003).

Garrison, D. *Church Planting Movements: How God Is Redeeming a Lost World* (Midlothian, VA: WIGTake Resources, 2004).

Gehring, R. W., *House Church and Mission: The Importance of Household Structures in Early Christianity* (Peabody, MA: Hendrickson, 2004).

Gerlach, L. P., and V. H. Hine. *People, Power, Change: Movements of Social Transformation* (Indianapolis: Bobbs-Merrill, 1970).

Gibbs, E., and R. K. Bolger. *Emerging Churches: Creating Christian Communities in Postmodern Cultures* (Grand Rapids: Baker Academic, 2006).

Gibbs, E., and I. Coffey. *Church Next: Quantum Changes in Christian Ministry* (Downers Grove, IL: InterVarsity, 2000).

Godin, S. *Survival Is Not Enough: Zooming, Evolution, and the Future of Your Company* (New York: Free Press, 2002).

————. *Unleashing the Ideavirus* (Dobbs Ferry, NY: Do You Zoom, 2000).

Guder, D. *The Incarnation and the Church's Witness* (Harrisburg, PA: Trinity, 1999).

———— (ed.). *Missional Church: A Vision for the Sending of the Church in North America* (Grand Rapids: Eerdmans, 1998).

Hall, D. J. *The End of Christendom and the Future of Christianity* (Harrisburg, PA: Trinity, 1997).

Hamilton, C., and R. D. *Affluenza: When Too Much Is Never Enough* (Crows Nest, NSW, Aus.: Allen & Unwin, 2005).

Hollenwager, W. J. "From Azusa Street to the Toronto Phenomena: Historical Roots of the Pentecostal Movement, *Concilium 3*, ed. Juergen Moltmann and Karl-Josef Kuschel (1996), 3, quoted in Veli-Matti Karkkainen, "Pentecostal Missiology in Ecumenical Perspective: Contributions, Challenges, Controversies," in *International Review of Mission* 88 (July 1999), 207 (whole article 207–25).

Hunter, G. G. III. *To Spread the Power: Church Growth in the Wesleyan Spirit* (Nashville: Abingdon, 1987).

Hurst, D. K. *Crisis and Renewal* (Cambridge: Harvard Business School Press, 2002).

Inchausti, R. *Subversive Orthodoxy: Rebels, Revolutionaries, and Other Christians in Disguise* (Grand Rapids: Brazos Press, 2005).

Johnson, S. *Emergence: The Connected Lives of Ants, Brains, Cities, and Software* (London: Penguin, 2001).

Kelly, G. *RetroFuture: Rediscovering Our Roots, Recharting Our Routes* (Downers Grove, IL: InterVarsity, 1999).

Kelly, J. *Consumerism* (Cambridge: Grove Books, 2003).

Kreider, A. *The Change of Conversion and the Origin of Christendom* (Harrisburg, PA: Trinity, 1999).

Kuhn, T. *The Structure of Scientific Revolutions*, 3rd ed. (Chicago: University of Chicago Press, 1996).

Lambert, T. *China's Christian Missions: The Costly Revival* (London: Monarch, 1999).

————. *The Resurrection of the Chinese Church* (London: Hodder & Stoughton, 1991).

Langmead, R. *The Word Made Flesh: Towards an Incarnational Missiology* (Lanham, MD: University Press of America, 2004).

Lewis, C. S. "Tolkien's Lord of the Rings," in *Essay Collection and Other Short Pieces* (London: HarperCollins, 2000).

Lyall, L. *The Phoenix Rises: The Phenomenal Growth of Eight Chinese Churches* (Singapore: OMF Books, 1992).

McGavran, D. *The Bridges of God: A Study in the Strategy of Missions* (London: World Dominion Press, 1955).

McLaren, B. *The Church on the Other Side: Doing Ministry in the Postmodern Matrix* (Grand Rapids: Zondervan, 2000).

MacQuarrie, J. *Principles of Christian Theology* (London: SCM, 1966).

Mihata, K. "The Persistence of 'Emergence,'" in R. A. Eve, S. Horsfall, and M. E. Lee (eds.), *Chaos, Complexity, and Sociology: Myths, Models, and Theories* (Thousand Oaks, CA: Sage, 1997).

Miller, V. J. *Consuming Religion: Christian Faith and Practice in a Consumer Culture* (New York: Continuum, 2004).

Murray, S. *Church Planting: Laying Foundations* (Carlisle: Paternoster, 1998).

———. *Post-Christendom: Church and Mission in a Strange New World* (Carlisle: Paternoster, 2004).

Nacpil, E. P. *Jesus' Strategy for Social Transformation* (Nashville: Abingdon, 1998).

Niebuhr, H. R. *Radical Monotheism and Western Culture* (online e-text available from www.religion-online.org/).

Pascale, R. T. *Managing on the Edge: How Successful Companies Use Conflict to Stay Ahead* (London: Viking, 1990).

Pascale, R. T., M. Millemann, L. Gioja. *Surfing the Edge of Chaos: The Laws of Nature and the New Laws of Business* (New York: Three Rivers Press, 2000).

Patzia, A. G. *The Emergence of the Church: Context, Growth, Leadership & Worship* (Downers Grove, IL: InterVarsity, 2001).

Peters, T. *Thriving on Chaos: Handbook for a Management Revolution* (London: Pan, 1987).

Peterson, J. *Church without Walls: Moving beyond Traditional Boundaries* (Colorado Springs: Navpress, 1992).

Peterson, J., and M. Shamy. *The Insider: Bringing the Kingdom of God into Your Everyday World* (Colorado Springs: Navpress, 2003).

Popper, K. *The Open Society and Its Enemies.* Vol. 1, *Plato* (London: Routledge, 1966).

Robinson, M., and Q. Smith. *Invading Secular Space: Strategies for Tomorrow's Church* (Grand Rapids: Kregel, 2003).

Roxburgh, A. J. *The Missionary Congregation, Leadership, & Liminality* (Harrisburg, PA: Trinity, 1997).

Roxburgh, A. J., and F. Romanuk. "Christendom Thinking to Missional Imagination: Leading the Cultivation of Missional Congregations" (unpublished manuscript, 2004).

Rushkoff, D. *Children of Chaos: Surviving the End of the World as We Know It* (London: Flamingo, 1997).

Rutba House (ed.). *Schools for Conversion: 12 Marks of a New Monasticism* (Eugene, OR: Cascade, 2005).

Snyder, H. A. *The Community of the King* (Downers Grove, IL: InterVarsity, 1977).

————. *Decoding the Church: Mapping the DNA of Christ's Body* (Grand Rapids: Baker, 2002).

————. *New Wineskins: Changing the Man-Made Structures of the Church* (London: Marshall, Morgan and Scott, 1978).

Stark, R. *The Rise of Christianity: How the Obscure, Marginal Jesus Movement Became the Dominant Religious Force in the Western World in a Few Centuries* (San Francisco: HarperCollins: 1996).

Stern, J. *Terror in the Name of God: Why Religious Militants Kill* (New York: HarperCollins, 2003).

Taylor, J. V. *The Christlike God* (London: SCM, 1992).

Turner, V. "Passages, Margins, and Poverty: Religious Symbols of *Communitas*," part 1. *Worship* 46 (1972): 390–412.

————. *The Ritual Process* (Ithaca, NY: Cornell University Press, 1969).

Vaus, W. *Mere Theology: A Guide to the Thought of C. S. Lewis* (Downers Grove, IL: InterVarsity, 2004).

Wallis, A. *The Radical Christian* (Columbia, MO: Cityhill, 1987).

Ward, P. *Liquid Church* (Peabody, MA: Hendrickson, 2002).

Webber, R. E. *The Younger Evangelicals: Facing the Challenges of the New World* (Grand Rapids: Baker, 2002).

Wheatley, M. *Leadership and the New Science: Discovering Order in a Chaotic World* (San Francisco: Berrett-Koehler, 1999).

Winter, R., and S. Hawthorne (eds.). *Perspectives on the World Christian Movement: A Reader* (Pasadena, CA: William Carey Library, 1999).

Yancey, Philip. "Discreet and Dynamic: Why, With No Apparent Resources, Chinese Churches Thrive," *Christianity Today*, July 2004, vol. 48, no. 7, 72.

Also by Alan Hirsh

THE FORGOTTEN WAYS
Reactivating the Missional Church

Alan Hirsch is convinced that the inherited formulas for growing the Body of Christ do not work anymore. Rather than relying on slightly revised solutions from the past, he sees a vision of the future growth of the church coming about by harnessing the power of the early church. *The Forgotten Ways* explores the concept of Apostolic Genius as a way to understand what caused the church to expand at various times in history, interpreting it for use in our own time and place.

"The global mission community is indebted to Hirsch for this seminal book. It is packed with solid exegesis and theological reflection and provides a fresh reading of contemporary Christian authors and a careful evaluation of paradigm-shifting authors from the leadership field. There is rich insight in each chapter for field practitioners and a fresh synthesis of the essentials of biblical missiology."—**Steve Hoke**, *Evangelical Missions Quarterly*

"Captivating . . . Hirsch creates novel terms, repackages discarded or unfamiliar words, and peppers the book with acronyms . . . This is a powerful book that will provoke a lot of helpful thought."— **Chad Hall**, *Leadership Journal*

"Hirsch presents a thoughtful reflection on how the Church might reconstruct itself in our current postmodern context while offering numerous insights that will be useful to those working in postmodern situations."—**Gary McIntosh**, *Outreach*

"[Hirsch's] reflections are worth reading, reading again, and most importantly acting upon. *The Forgotten Ways* is a welcome and significant addition to the literature on mission to the West written by a leading missiological strategist. It will prove to be a useful tool to help shape new forms of missional church—for church planters, those leading change in existing churches and all mission-hearted followers of Jesus."—**Darren Cronshaw**, *Journal of the American Society for Church Growth*

"Alan Hirsch's inspiring work in *The Forgotten Ways* delivers for those interested in rekindling the heart of every successful church movement . . . Hirsch proposes no less than a complete, grassroots, put-up-or-shut-up, no holds barred, pull-out-all-the-stops reassembling of how we do church. But he makes it look possible."—**Luke Trouten**, *YouthWorker Journal*